Twenty-Somethings

This is a work of fiction. All the characters, organizations, and events portrayed in this novel are either products of the authors imagination or used fictitiously.

Chapter 1

It was 7:45 Monday morning at the Coffee Hole. People were spread out across the shop trying to get to work, enjoy their morning, or just get home to get some rest.

"Your total is $5.31," Kelsey said as a customer swiped their debit card and quickly gathered their items. "Thank you!" she added with a smile as the customer turned to leave.

Her hair was barely holding its shape as the bun she made las night began to fall apart. She had shoulder length dirty blonde hair and green eyes. She had a slim figure, and was average height for a girl in her twenties.

After helping the last customer in line, she turned to an older man stocking milk into the fridge behind the counter. He was in his late thirties with short brown hair and brown eyes, his face made him look older than he really was.

"Tom when can I get out of here? I'm dying!" Kelsey smiled as she collapsed on to the counter.

"Amanda should be here soon. I guess I could cover until she gets here," Tom replied.

"Yes!" Kelsey said with a loud sigh and a smile. "You're the best boss ever," she continued as she gathered her things.

"Yea, most bosses wouldn't do this ya know," Tom replied with a playful bravado.

"I'll remember it next time I need to come in on my day off," Kelsey fired back with a smile.

Tom smiled back. "Thank you. Now go get some rest."

"Yea maybe an hour or two before class," she said with a sigh. She was already at the door of the shop.

"I don't know how you do it," Tom shouted to her.

"Lots of coffee," Kelsey laughed as she left the shop and headed home.

Kelsey returned home later that day after her classes to find her roommate just waking up.

"It's four in the afternoon Ashley. What are you doing with your life?" Kelsey asked as she put some left over food in the microwave.

2

"Well I was enjoying it until *somebody* came home and started slamming doors and turning on lights," Ashley replied with some serious sass.

Ashley was a little bit shorter than Kelsey with brown wavy hair and green eyes. Most would say her body type had all the right stuff in all the right places.

"Don't you have class today?" Kelsey asked.

Ashley smiled. "I did, butttt, I turned work in early, so I don't have to go."

"Your gonna fail that class again," Kelsey laughed.

Ashley stopped. "How could you say that!" she asked with a laugh.

"I'm barely passing it and I actually show up every day," Kelsey replied.

"Yea, but you have it in the morning. Dr. Green is a dick, Dr. Cass is great. She won't fail me; besides, I have all the work from last year. I'm set."

"If I'm ever dying I really hope you're not the nurse that is working with me," Kelsey said.

"That hurts," Ashley laughed. "Just remember though, when it's all done we will have the same degree."

"I still wonder why you want to be a nurse," Kelsey replied.

"It was this or cosmetology," Ashley explained, "and last time I cut my brothers hair we had to shave his head," she laughed.

"I can not believe you just said that," Kelsey laughed. "You don't think that there are *any* other jobs out there?"

"Anyywayyy!" Ashley laughed as she took a piece of Kelsey's chicken. "You coming out tonight?"

"Sorry can't," Kelsey replied.

"Why not?"

"Wellll I have work tomorrow morning."

"We won't be out late."

"Anddd I have a date with interflix"

"Oh my god. All you do is watch tv and work," Ashley said with frustrated exhale.

"Anddd it would require me to be around people, so definitely no," Kelsey said seriously

"You're going to die an old cat lady," Ashley warned.

"But at least I will have true love in my cats. How many boyfriends is that this year?" Kelsey asked.

"Oh my god! You're such a bitch," Ashley laughed. "And it's only been three. How am I supposed to know they will all turn out to be douchebags?" she asked seriously.

"I don't know," Kelsey paused, "maybe by the douche tattoos, douche clothes, douche cars, anger issues, trying to fuck you on the first date, the list goes on."

"I can't believe you would stereotype somebody by the way they dress, act, or even by their tattoos. I try to get to know the real them," Ashley explained confidently.

4

"Yeaaa, the real them," Kelsey said as she pushed her tongue into her cheek while waving her fist in front of her mouth.

"OH MY GOD!" Ashley laughed as she pushed Kelsey.

They both laughed, and Kelsey stood up and went to her room after throwing away her trash. She changed into a pair of thick pajama pants and a big tee shirt before nestling into her bed with two blankets and a small army of pillows. She turned on a TV series about serial killers and watched it until falling asleep.

Chapter 2

The alarm clock rang at 4:30 waking Ryan up for work.

"Please tell me a hail storm came through and were off today," he groaned as he rolled out of bed.

After just standing in the hot water for twenty minutes he got dressed. Ryan was just over six feet tall and barely in his twenties. He had short brown hair and blue eyes with soft features that didn't compliment his large arms and the first signs of a beer gut.

Ryan met his father in the kitchen.

Stan was a big man with short brown hair and a built physique. His face was half hidden with a short beard and mustache combo.

"It's about time," Stan said as he ate a bowl of eggs and syrup. "Thought you might have died in the shower."

"If only," Ryan laughed.

"It's supposed to be 97 today," Stan warned.

"No worse than any other day," Ryan laughed. "Maybe all the equipment will go down and I get go home."

"You keep wishing that until you end up jobless and homeless," Stan replied seriously.

"I know, I know," Ryan said as he grabbed a bagel and walked toward the door.

"I've got a full pot of coffee right here," Stan said. "If you didn't waste your time and money on that place you might be able to get a real breakfast."

"Love you Dad!" Ryan said casually dismissing the advice as he walked out the door.

Stan sighed and shook his head. "Love you too."

Ryan walked into the The Coffee Hole and took a big sniff with a satisfying exhale. He looked around as he started towards the counter. The shop was quiet save for the soft sound of the new age jazz coming from the speakers. The sun hadn't rose yet, and the world seemed to be at peace.

"You know I can't help you if it's cold," Kelsey said as she put a cup of coffee on the counter. "Your late."

"I know," Ryan smiled. "Just didn't want to wake up this morning." He handed her the exact change for the drink.

"How's work been? I haven't seen you in about a week," Kelsey asked.

"Not bad. Same old stuff different day. I did notice you haven't been here over nights in a while," he replied.

"Yea we had a guy quit so I've been all over the place trying to cover shifts," Kelsey explained.

"Damn," Ryan sighed. "I may have to work outside but somehow I feel like you got it worse. You're in school aren't you?"

"Yea for nursing,"

"Oh, so you're gonna be a doctor?" Ryan laughed.

Kelsey scoffed. "Yea right. I just want to help people, I'm barely making this work," she laughed.

Ryan looked around. "One thing I do envy is that you get to enjoy the night. Closest thing I get are these mornings."

"Don't worry it's not all that exciting," she assured him.

"Well I'm not looking for all that," he added, "it's peaceful."

Kelsey paused for a second, lost in thought then snapped back and replied. "Sorry," she laughed.

"No worries," Ryan said with a smile. "It was nice to see you again. Good luck with your schooling."

"Thanks! Don't work too hard today," Kelsey replied.

"I never do," Ryan said with a slick smile as he went to find a seat and relax before he had to be at the job site.

Ryan walked up to the half-built hotel building to meet a group of guys wearing hard hats standing around a water cooler.

"Morning guys," he said.

"Morning," Luis and Jerry replied.

"Alright, so honestly," Jerry started.

"Uh-oh..." Ryan said as he rubbed his forehead.

"Come on just listen," Jerry insisted with a smile. Jerry was in his forties and was a few inches shorter than Ryan. He was a bald man with tan white skin, a beer gut, and various faded tattoos. "Ok, so would you fuck that fat bitch that works for the insurance place?" he asked.

"I don't even know who you're talking about," Ryan replied.

"The one with the black hair that wears dresses that are too tight and no panties," Jerry explained.

"You mean Samantha?" Ryan asked. "She's not insurance, she works for the city."

"Uh-oh! He knows her name and her job!" Luis said getting excited.

"So your saying you would?" Jerry asked.

"No, I'm not saying that," Ryan defended.

"Even if you were drunk?" Luis asked.

Luis was a Mexican man in his twenties that stood almost as tall as Ryan. He had tan skin and wore his hair short and spiked up.

"No," Ryan said, and the two others erupted with boos and jeers.

"No way! You know you'd do it if nobody knew," Luis insisted.

Ryan laughed. "Do you have any idea how early it is for this?"

"He's changing the subject! I knew it!" Luis said as he hit Jerry in the shoulder.

Ryan was about to defend himself before Stan called everybody for a meeting. The men all gathered around him.

"Ayy pelón! What are you and your girlfriends laughing about over there?" Ranchero asked Jerry as the approached.

"Eatin' your mom's ass last night!" Jerry replied as he grabbed the air in front of him with both hands and flicked his tongue.

"Eww bro! You know his mom doesn't wipe!" a voice added from the crowd and all the men started laughing and going back and forth with jokes.

"Alright, everybody, calm down," Stan said just loud enough to get the situation under control. "We all know were behind on schedule. This is gonna be a long one, I want all of you to pick up where you left off yesterday." He then repeated all the information in Spanish. "I'll get back with you guys at lunch if anything changes."

The men all started to disperse and went to start work.

"That still gets me that your dad knows Spanish like that," Jerry said to Ryan.

"Way he sees it, is if half of his employees speak a certain language he needs to know how to talk to them," Ryan explained.

"Makes sense. A lot of the guys do seem to like him, so I guess he's doing something right," Jerry said.

Chapter 3

The alarm clock rang, and Gerome half pulled himself out of bed. He sat on the edge of the bed for a minute or two rubbing his eyes. He was a young black man in his twenties with very short hair that was trimmed to perfection. He was skinny; however, his muscles were toned, showing his commitment to his trips to the gym. After a quick shower he put on one of his suits from the collection in his closet. After struggling with his tie for almost five minutes he let out a sharp sigh.

"Not today," Gerome said as he threw the tie on his bed. He grabbed a clip on from his dresser and quickly fastened it.

Gerome lived in a nice one-bedroom apartment right outside of the center of the city. The living room had all the furniture it needed however it looked empty. Each room lacked any personal touches and almost resembled the type of place you would see in a magazine for new homes.

After a quick bowl of cereal Gerome grabbed his things and left for work.

After his normal morning coffee trip to The Coffee Hole Gerome pulled up to a huge building with 'Whits Financial' written on the side. He made his way in and headed to the elevator. After reaching his floor he slowly walked to his desk.

"Morning Gerome," Carver said as Gerome walked past his desk.

"Morning," Gerome replied with a smile.

"Morning," Stacey said as she walked to the break room.

"Morning," Gerome replied again.

The usual greetings carried on until Gerome got to his desk. He sat down and started looking over his folders to try and see what he needed to do first. He stacked all his papers in a specific order and began to work.

Lunch time came, and everybody chatted about what to eat or office gossip.

"You coming to the office party this weekend Gerome?" Carver asked as they were walking to the break room.

"I wouldn't miss it," Gerome replied. "Gonna be some big executives there."

"Always thinking ahead," Carver said. "I just want the free food and drinks." he continued with a laugh.

Carver was an Italian man in his forties with dark brown eyes. He had a belly and wore his medium length black hair slicked back.

"You're a mess," Gerome laughed.

"Ayy!" Carver protested with a laugh. "If they wanna give me free stuff I'm gonna take it. After all the work I do, I'm not letting this get away."

"Some days are harder than others," Gerome added.

"You boys still complaining about being on the bottom?" A voice asked from behind them. "Kidding kidding!" the voice laughed.

"Well Bradley, you know getting on your knees looks good for the boss, but I can't say I agree with your five-year plan," Carver replied with a smirk.

Anger flashed on Bradley's face for a second before he gained his composure. He was a young man, not a day past twenty-two, with light brown hair and grayish eyes. His sharp features were made less prevalent by skin that was as pale as you would expect for a person who never spent time outside.

"Kidding kidding," Carver added with a quick laugh and pat on Bradley's shoulder.

"Very funny," Bradley replied. "Just remember the higher-ups hear and see more than you think. You've got potential Gerome, just watch out who you surround yourself with."

With that Bradley left and the two returned to their break.

"Guys such an asshole because his dad is some big shot at a well-known bank or something," Carver said.

"It is funny, I think he started here after I did and way after you," Gerome added.

"Yea, but kissing ass and paying for promotions isn't hard for that guy," Carver replied.

Gerome sighed. "I've had to do my fair share of ass kissing."

Carver laughed. "He does have a point, I heard that some of the department heads have their eyes on you."

"Hopefully I'll be running this place one day," Gerome laughed

"Yea then I can ride your coat tails straight to the top!" Carver laughed as he elbowed Gerome.

"As long as I can make this dream a reality I don't mind taking you with me," Gerome said with laugh.

Chapter 4

Light creaked through the blinds of the apartment's window to barely illuminate the room. The room was littered with paint brushes, clothes, canvases, drawings, and all other assortment of scattered artist tools.

With a yawn and a sigh Alex rolled over and looked at his phone, the time read 12:47. With a groan he got out of bed and got ready for the day. His hair was a twisted mass of blonde dreads that hung to his shoulders. His skin was slightly tan for someone who got minimal sun and it matched his light blue eyes. He was tall but by no means a towering man in his mid-twenties. After standing in front of the mirror in a daze for a moment he brushed his teeth and got dressed. He grabbed a couple of paintings and some supplies, putting them in his bag and leaving the apartment.

Alex arrived at the coffee hole midafternoon. He walked in with a big smile and greeted the regulars and staff he knew.

"Hey Kelsey!" he said as he walked to the counter.

"Hey Alex!" she replied with a smile. "The usual or are you feeling adventurous today?"

"The usual," he said with a laugh. "Gotta save up my adventure for something big."

"You got it," she replied as she made him a cup of iced coffee with caramel.

"Is Tom here?" Alex asked.

"Yea he should be back any minute," Kelsey replied.

Almost as if he heard them Tom walked into the shop. Alex turned to greet him.

"Tom! I've got a new painting for you!" Alex said with excitement.

"Oh no…" Tom shook his head and sighed then laughed. "I already told you, I bought just one. I've got no space for another."

"You could put this one right over there!" Alex protested as he pointed to a blank space on the wall.

"That area has to be blank for the room to mesh. I can't ruin my atmosphere with a million paintings," Tom explained.

"Paintings are atmosphere!" Alex replied.

Tom shook his head. "I'm gonna have to start having the police ready to stop this awful soliciting."

"You really are the worst," Alex said with a seriously concerned tone. "Are you sure you're ok? To hate art really is unheard of."

"I love art! I happen to have visited some of the finest are museums in the world," Tom said proudly.

"And you still can't see the beauty right before your eyes," Alex said with a sad tone then smiled. "It's ok! I'll come back tomorrow."

"You better not," Tom said seriously and walked into his office.

"He'll come around," Alex assured Kelsey with a smile.

"Sure," Kelsey laughed. "I mean he has to eventually right?"

"Exactly!" Alex replied. "You understand. So what's new? Watch an entire tv series in one weekend again?" Alex laughed.

"Hey!" Kelsey defended. "That was a good series!" she sighed. "But no, I have been really busy with school and work my TV time is suffering," she frowned. "Anything that cuts into my shows really needs to be reconsidered on whether or not it's actually important," she laughed.

"Who needs school," Alex laughed.

"Yea," Kelsey laughed. "Why can't I get paid for watching TV and being tired. I'd be rich."

"If only," Alex replied with a smile.

"It will be all worth it in the end," Kelsey said. "Or at least that's the plan," she laughed.

"I hope so," Alex said. "You can do it!"

"Thank you!" Kelsey said

"Don't work too hard," Alex said as he got ready to leave.

"You too," Kelsey replied. "Bye."

"Bye," Alex said with a big grin and a wave, as he walked to the door.

Chapter 5

Class let out early for Kelsey and Ashley. They walked to their cars through the campus grounds.

"You staying home all night again?" Ashley asked.

Kelsey laughed. "No, I actually have work tonight."

"You work too much. When are you gonna quit that place?" Ashley asked.

"Unlike you, I have to pay my bills," Kelsey joked.

"I work! And pay bills!" Ashley defended. "I just don't kill myself with school and work. If I get into trouble I can always ask my mom for help I don't mind. They are happy to help me make it through."

"I can't do that. Your just not supposed to. Were supposed to be adults now," Kelsey said seriously.

"You mean your dad wouldn't help you if you asked?" Ashley countered.

"He would do anything if I asked probably. He always asks if I'm ok and if I need anything, and tells me how proud of me he is that I got a scholarship. That's honestly the only reason I can even be here. I can't afford these classes alone," Kelsey explained.

"I don't think anyone can afford these classes," Ashley laughed. "I'm gonna be in debt forever by the time I get this degree."

"Not if you just studied more and didn't have to retake classes," Kelsey laughed.

"Hey! Those were back when I had my scholarship, so they were free!" Ashley protested and stuck her tongue out at Kelsey.

"You're a mess," Kelsey smiled.

"Oh yea," Ashley agreed. "But aren't we all?"

"Yea," Kelsey looked up. "I'm just ready for life to get easier. It will be nice when I can be done with school and this crazy work schedule and start at a hospital."

"I'm ready to meet my hot doctor so I don't have to work!"
Ashley laughed.

Kelsey turned to her. "Oh my god!"

"I'm just kidding!" Ashley laughed.

It was a fairly slow night at The Coffee Hole as Kelsey sat behind the counter chatting with customers.

"… It's really cool how it works. The temperatures are just perfect for them to grow there. If the soil was even a tiny bit cooler or warmer they wouldn't grow," Kelsey explained.

"That's amazing," an old woman replied.

"You really are the greatest cashier I've ever met," The older gentleman with her added. "You really care about your customers and always have such interesting things to tell."

Kelsey laughed slightly. "Thank you. If only everyone thought so. Some customers can be…" she paused, "… difficult."

"Oh, don't let it worry you sweetie. Everything in life has its ups and downs, it's about if your happy and most importantly, making others happy," the woman replied.

"Thank you, Mrs. Trover," Kelsey said.

"Well I guess we should get out of here. We don't want to hold up the line," the gentleman smiled and winked at Kelsey. "Don't work too hard."

"I'll try," Kelsey smiled and waved. "Have a good night!"

"You too," the couple replied in unison.

"I don't think anybody is happy here," Jason added with a smirk as he stocked things behind the counter.

"It's not so bad," Kelsey said. "If I didn't have school I could do this for a while I think."

Jason looked stunned. "Forget that. This place is just some job."

"I like talking to people and seeing all the smiles," Kelsey explained. "It doesn't even feel like work some nights."

"Whatever you say," Jason replied.

Chapter 6

Ryan drove down the road blasting music and joyfully anticipating the party. Luis rode in the passenger seat as they approached a long line of parked cars and stopped at the end of them.

"Guess we found it," Ryan laughed.

"Helll yea!" Luis said. "There's gotta be so many sexy bitches here."

"Just don't start any fights," Ryan laughed. "I don't want to have to leave early."

"Ay, I never start a fight, I just gotta finish em when dudes act up," Luis replied.

"You don't have to finish anything," Ryan noted.

"Shit, and let some punk just disrespect me? Fuck that shit," Luis replied as he hopped out of the truck.

Ryan laughed. "Yea guess you're right."

Both floors of the house had people scattered around dancing, talking, and playing a variety of drinking games.

"Ayy!" cheers came from friends as the two made their way in.

"Beer's in the fridge!" a voice shouted.

"Yea!" Ryan cheered and went to grab one.

The night carried on with more drinks and games.

"I swear I can do it! I do it all the time at work with steel rods!" Ryan defended as he held a broken broom handle from an earlier stunt. Stumbling back and forth he tried to balance it on his forehead. He immediately dropped it every time and everyone watching burst into laughter.

"Just stop man you're gona hurt yourself," Luis laughed as he stumbled and caught himself on Ryan's shoulder.

"You've seen me do it! Tell em," Ryan told Luis.

"I don't know, I don't remember," Luis laughed as he moved back to the wall.

"You're a bastard!" Ryan laughed. "I could do it if I wasn't drunk." He turned and grabbed a beer, chugging what was left of it, he crushed the can and threw the broom on the floor. "Fuck this, I'm going to bed," he laughed. After stumbling his way to Luis, he hugged him. "Love you man! This really is the life!"

"Love you too bro!" Luis said and turned to a few random people. "You fuck with this guy I'll whoop your ass!"

The two young men stumbled and started to fall. Each one used the other to try and maintain balance only making it worse as the crashed to the ground. After laughing for minutes, they both stumbled their way to the living room to pass out.

Chapter 7

Gerome got ready for the night. He made sure everything he was going to wear was ironed and brushed it all with a lint roller.

"God I hate this," he said to himself as he made sure everything checked out. "I need that promotion," he added as he added a small spray of cologne to his wrists.

Gerome walked up to the entrance of a nice restaurant.

"I'm sorry the restaurant has been reserved for Whits employees," the doorman informed a couple in front of him.

The man looked very upset as he stormed off with his wife making comments about the restaurant.

Gerome approached the door.

"I'm sorry sir the restaurant has been reserved by..." the doorman started.

Before he could finish Gerome took out his invitation and handed it to him.

"I'm sorry sir. Right this way," the doorman apologized.

Gerome nodded to him and walked into the restaurant. He found his way to familiar faces after a minute or two. Carver was finding seat at a booth next to the bar when Gerome joined him.

"Hey man," Gerome said. "You see the bosses yet?"

"Nah, I figure they will make some grand entrance to boost their egos," Carver scoffed.

"Yea, that doesn't seem too unreasonable," Gerome replied.

After most people had found a seat a voice came from the speakers and the soft music stopped.

"Thank you all for attending this dinner! We want nothing more than to show our appreciation for our employees. Before we get started we would like to take a moment to introduce some of our most influential members. Our president: Mr. Whits." The old man came out and waved at the people. Our vice president: Mr. Strider..." the list went on as the executives all entered and found their seats at a specially reserved table in the middle of the restaurant.

After the introductions were over the service staff came alive and began to move from table to table getting orders and bringing drinks.

"I'll take the biggest glass of wine you have and some mozzarella sticks," Carver told the waiter with a smile.

"Yes sir. Not a problem. For you sir?" he asked Gerome.

"Just some water is fine," Gerome replied.

"Yes sir," and the waiter left.

"You have to be kidding me," Carver said. "An open bar and any food you want, and you get water?"

"I need to be focused. This could be my chance to get my foot in the door with the executives," Gerome explained.

"Man, you really care about this promotion," Carver replied.

"This job is all that matters. This is my chance to make it in the world," Gerome said.

Carver laughed. "Look around you. We already made it. The only difference from us to them is a nicer house and car," he gestured toward the executive table. "We all make enough to live comfortably. Hell, if anything we got it better off. Less responsibility is nice, all that money isn't worth it in my book."

"It's not just the money..." Gerome paused. "I don't know. It's just something that's important, being successful."

"You get offered free booze and food and you can't enjoy it," Carver laughed. "That doesn't sound like winning to me."

Gerome laughed. "That's only for now. Once I'm on top I can do whatever I want."

As the night went on the president and some other higher ups made their rounds and greeted the employees. They made it to Gerome and Carver.

"Evening boys," Whits said with a big smile.

"Good evening Mr. President," Gerome replied.

"Melton? That's it, isn't it?" Mr. Whits asked.

"Yes sir," Gerome stood up. "Gerome Melton," he offered his hand to shake.

"Call me David," Mr. Whits said and shook Gerome's hand. "I've heard a lot about your work and I'm impressed. The competition is tough, but you remain ahead of the pack. Keep it up."

"Thank you Mr. Whits," Gerome replied and sat back down.

"You enjoying yourself as always Mr. Romano?" Whits laughed.

"You know it sir," Carver laughed. "Thank you again for the night."

"Any time, we just want our employees to feel valued," Mr. Whits said with a big smile. "You gentlemen enjoy your night," and he left to the next table.

Carver laughed. "Fucking prick."

"What are you talking about?" Gerome asked.

"I've been here a long time. They don't value us. We make a thousand they make a million. Didn't you see that shit eating grin on his face?" Carver asked.

"He looked happy?" Gerome replied.

"Don't let them fool you," Carver warned. "They want you to feel like that, so you will work harder for no pay raise."

Gerome laughed. "I think you've had too many."

"Just wait and see," Carver said with a smile.

"Whatever you say," Gerome replied casually dismissing the man with a smile. "It's not easy, but the extra work does pay off eventually."

Chapter 8

Alex loaded up paintings into the back of his beat up old station wagon. After packing up and making a short drive he was at the local flea market. He pulled up next to an empty stall and began to unpack.

"Morning Alex," a woman called from the stall next to him.

"Morning Pam," he called back. "I'm feeling good about today."

"That's good. I hope you sell a lot today," Pam said with a smile.

"Thanks!" Alex replied.

The morning carried on and Alex sold a few paintings. After a while a young man walked up to the stall dressed in a nice pair of jeans and a button up shirt.

"Good morning," Alex said. "What are you looking for today?"

"Honestly, I don't know," Gerome replied. "I need to fill my empty walls in my apartment."

"Well what do you like? I can let you know if I have anything in that style," Alex informed him.

Gerome sighed and slightly laughed. "I don't even know man. It seems like I don't like anything anymore."

"Well the thing about having a painting in your house is that it should reflect a part of you and help identify your home as yours," Alex said.

"That's deep. I was just thinking about getting some fruit in a bowl or something," Gerome laughed.

"It's totally deep man," Alex replied in a slow dragged tone as he barely held his eyes open. Gerome laughed, and Alex returned to normal. "But honestly, you really need to think about it. Art shouldn't be a waste of space or filler."

"Hmm…" Gerome said as he scanned the paintings.

"I'll tell you what. You seem to have forgotten who you are. Take some time to think about it, and when you find it, I'll paint you something free of charge," Alex offered.

"I didn't forget who I am," Gerome laughed. "I just don't know what I want on a painting."

"You don't have any hobbies or anything that inspires you?" Alex asked. "I know you had to have something when you were a kid. You forgot it. You forgot who you were."

"We all had hobbies as a kid," Gerome replied. "I can't get some child's cartoon or dinosaurs on a painting," he laughed. "You lose those as you grow up."

"But you don't lose who you are," Alex said. "I know it's philosophy coming from some white dude with dreads in a dirty flea market stall," he laughed, "but trust me. I'm not as totally crazy."

"I might get busy and not come back for a long time," Gerome warned.

"I don't expect you to find yourself in a weekend," Alex smiled. "Just don't forget to come back when you do."

Gerome stared at him for a second. "Ok man, whatever you say. By the way what's your name?"

"Alex Rings," Alex said.

"Gerome Melton," Gerome said as he extended his hand to shake. The two shook hands. "I guess I'll see you around?"

"Yes sir," Alex said with a smile and the two parted ways.

Gerome stopped at the end of the walk way that held all the market stalls. "Now what am I supposed to do. I still haven't found anything to put in the house." He stopped and thought for a second. "Guess I'll just come back for my free painting soon."

Chapter 9

A couple of months passed, and the fall semester started. Kelsey was staring at her laptop in her room sitting on her bed. She stopped staring and sighed as she pushed the laptop away.

"Ugh." Kelsey said as she walked to the kitchen. "Maybe there's something new in here," she mused as she opened the fridge and stared blankly. "I hate everything…" she said as she rested her head on the freezer door.

After making her way back to her room she face-planted on her bed. After laying there for minutes she got up and changed clothes. The new outfit went from pajama pants and a large tee shirt, to sweat pants and a slightly smaller tee shirt.

"Ahh! It's alive!" a voice shouted as Kelsey walked in the door of The Coffee Hole.

"Very funny Michael," she replied sad voice and a smile.

"Aww, what's wrong? School?" Michael asked.

"Yea. This project is kicking my ass," Kelsey explained.

"Something had to be wrong to see you in public outside of school and work," Michael laughed.

"I need some coffee and some food," Kelsey said with a frown.

"Sure thing," he laughed. "Any requests?"

"Anything that gets this project done tonight," Kelsey replied.

"You're really doing the night before aren't you?" Michael asked with a serious voice.

"What!" Kelsey defended.

"I guarantee your teacher gave you that project weeks, or even months ago," Michael said.

"You're not making this any better!" Kelsey half laughed half cried.

Michael laughed. "Ok. Ok. Just go have a seat."

"Thank you…" she replied.

After paying for her food Kelsey sat down and enjoyed her meal. As she sipped on her coffee Alex walked in to the shop.

"Hey Kelsey," He said. "Care if I sit?"

"That's fine," she replied.

"What are you doing out?" Alex asked. "Can't sleep?"

"I guess you could say that," she scoffed. "I need to finish this project."

"Ohhh. Last minute?" Alex asked.

"Yeaaaa," Kelsey replied.

"Well you better get it done!" Alex said with a smile. "You got this. Just remember why you're doing this in the first place."

"Because I don't want to fail," Kelsey laughed.

Alex laughed. "Well yea… but I mean the degree as a whole. It's worth it, isn't it?" he asked.

"Well yea, I guess," she replied.

"You guess?" Alex asked. "The things we want and the goals we have need to be absolute. This is what keeps us going when it gets really hard," he smiled. "As long as you chase your dreams you can't lose."

"Why can't I just paint all the time like you?" Kelsey laughed. "That's the life."

"It's nice," Alex smiled, "but it has its problems. It's just what I love."

"Your dream is to just paint?" she asked.

"Yes and no," he replied. "It's to make the world see that you can do anything. People have this tendency to let the world tell them that they can't. They can't be an athlete, can't be a comedian, they can't be an archeologist, they can't be anything but what this world offers them. Not only am I going to be living proof that you can make it happen, I also want my paintings to inspire people to be what they were called to be. I know I have a gift and I won't let it go to waste no matter what."

"Wow," Kelsey said. "That's a big dream."

"Yea, but it's going one day at a time," Alex reassured them both.

"I wish I could be as happy and motivated as you," Kelsey said.

"You can!" Alex encouraged. "You just need to tap into it!"

"Maybe," Kelsey said skeptically. "The only thing I feel like tapping into, is a bottle of wine and my bed."

"You got this," Alex laughed and stood up. "Gotta run, but I'll see you around."

"Ok!" Kelsey said cheerfully as she waved. "Bye."

Chapter 10

Music roared from inside the house while indistinct conversations made for background noise. Ryan stepped out onto the back porch and closed the door muffling most of the noise. He took a seat, letting out a deep relaxing sigh and looked at the night sky.

After a short time, the door opened and quickly closed leaving the sound of a crying girl behind him. She walked to the railing of the porch before noticing Ryan.

"Oh my god," the girl said quickly wiping her eyes. "I'm so sorry."

"It's ok. Is everything alright?" Ryan asked.

"It's fine," she replied. "Just being a slut," she continued as the tears came back.

Ryan's eyes widened slightly showing some discomfort. "Woah hold on. Just relax. Here, have a seat," he said as he moved a chair for her to sit in.

She sat down, and Ryan introduced himself. "My names Ryan," he said as he sat back in his chair.

"I'm Lindsey," she replied fighting back the tears again.

She was a young girl in her early twenties with blonde hair and green eyes. She was pretty, even after crying, and the lack of make-up showed in the absence of a mess on her face that was indicative of smeared make-up.

"What happened?" Ryan asked and caught himself quickly. "I mean… if you don't mind talking," he added.

"My boyfriend just makes me feel like shit for doing anything," she said as she looked at the neighbor's house. "'Oh, you wanna fuck him now?', 'You love dancing for all those guys, don't you?', 'Why don't you just text that guy you were fucking at work?', it never fucking stops!" she said angrily. "I've never done anything like that," she added as the tears came back in full force. "I've cut people off, I've cancelled plans, I've done so much to prove that I'm a good girlfriend."

"I'm sorry," Ryan said with a small silence after.

Lindsey wiped the tears again and quickly calmed down some. "No, I'm sorry. You don't even know me and I'm just blowing up on you, throwing all my problems in your face."

Ryan laughed. "Well I guess you could say I asked for it, couldn't you?"

"Yea... but still," she replied softening up a bit. "Hey, you're the broom handle guy, aren't you?"

Ryan stopped for a second and sighed with a smile. "Yeaaa. That's me."

Lindsey smiled.

Ryan rubbed his forehead before bouncing back. "Hey," he said as he scooted his chair closer to hers. "Look up right there," he said as he pointed to the sky. "Do you see that bright star with the two close to the left and right of it?"

She paused and looked for a second. After a couple of moments, she replied, "No," with a frown.

"Ok hold on," Ryan said as he focused and leaned forward. "Right there," he pointed with his arm held in front of her face. "A bright star with two close to the left and right."

"I think I see it..." she replied softly.

"Ok now connect them with that one farther down in a line, and connect the other two farther ones on the left and right up top. You should be able to see a really big bent T," Ryan explained.

Lindsey stared blankly for a minute before gasping. "Oh! I see it!"

"Try to imagine that T is a bird with the sides being wings. They say that that is the eagle that carried thunder bolts for Zeus," Ryan explained.

42

"I've never seen it before," she replied. "That's really cool." She paused. "I can find the big dipper sometimes," Lindsey laughed.

"Well there you go. That's something," Ryan smiled.

"So is this what you do? Come to parties and sit outside looking at stars?" Lindsey asked with a smile.

Ryan stumbled over his words for a second. "No, I was just getting some air and just happened to be here," he laughed.

"It's ok," Lindsey laughed. "It's pretty cool, and it helped me calm down a bit. Thank you."

"No problem," Ryan said blushing slightly. "Most people don't think it's that cool. It can be boring and hard to see them if you don't know where to look." He paused for a moment before getting back on track. "I can try to show you some more if you want?"

"We've already had sex anyway," she said sarcastically.

Ryan paused stunned for a second.

"I'm sorry," Lindsey laughed shaking her head. "Yea, that's fine."

"Now your boyfriend isn't gonna come kick the door open, is he?" Ryan asked. "I don't want to have to beat someone's ass tonight."

"He already left," she replied.

"He what?" Ryan asked. "Do you have a ride home?"

"Yea one of my friends is already on her way," Lindsey explained.

"Oh, ok. Well I guess I can get a little bit more of your time then," Ryan smiled.

Just then Lindsey's phone went off and she checked it.

"She's here." Lindsey stood up. "Thank you so much for talking to me."

Ryan stood up as well and Lindsey opened her arms to offer a hug. They hugged, and she thanked him again before turning to leave.

"Hey... uh," Ryan started to say as she reached the door. "In case you ever need to talk again or anything... you care if I give you my number?"

"Ok," she replied with a smile and took out her phone.

After giving her his number Lindsey left into the house and Ryan sat back down in his chair with a sigh and looked up at the sky.

Chapter 11

Gerome stood in line at The Coffee Hole to place an order. It was late in the evening Friday. The front door opened, and more customers walked in and took their place behind him. After paying and getting his order Gerome turned to leave.

"Woah G is that you?" the man behind Gerome in line asked.

"Dang!" Gerome replied. "It's been a long time."

"Yea it has," Demetry said. "What happened? How you been? Why is your hair so short?" he asked the last part with a smile.

Demetry was barely shorter than Gerome, with brown hair that he spiked up. His Russian accent wasn't very strong; however, it did show up when he spoke.

"Things are good," Gerome informed him, "and I have to have it for work."

"Oh yea. I forgot you got some masters in law or something," Demetry replied.

"If only," Gerome laughed. "It was a bachelors in accounting and human resources."

"Dang, so you work around here?" Demetry asked.

"Yea moved back late last year," Gerome said.

By this time the two had stepped out of line to make way for new customers.

"You should catch up with the guys! We had no idea you were back in town. Digs was just talking about you literally last week, no lie," Demetry said.

"Sorry," Gerome said. I just have to work a lot. Guess I forgot to hit everybody up. I don't really talk to anybody to be honest. Outside of work," He added.

"It's ok. It seems like you're doing well for yourself," Demetry assured him.

"Yea. How about you guys? What are you up too?" Gerome asked.

"Were all working at the pizza place right down the street for a steady income while we do shows," he explained.

"You're still in that band?" Gerome laughed.

"Dude we've done shows at a couple of bigger venues. It's slow but we are getting a name. We really need our lead guitar back though, this tool that is filling in isn't working out." Demetry laughed.

"Dang that sounds rough," Gerome said.

Demetry smiled. "I know you're a rich business man now, but I hope you will stop and see us. We work most weekend nights so come by the restaurant if you're free and we can catch up. It's right next to that yoga studio right before the four-way."

"Ok. Thanks man. It was really nice to see you again," Gerome said with a smile.

"You too man!" Demetry replied.

Gerome offered his hand to shake and it awkwardly turned into a fist bump after a couple of maneuvers to get there. They both laughed and Demetry got back in line, while Gerome left.

Chapter 12

Alex packed up his best paintings into his car with an excited smile.

"This is gonna be the one," he said as he closed the back-seat door.

After driving for a couple of hours he arrived at a big event center. Cars were scattered around the parking lot and people walked back and forth coming and going to the event. Alex grabbed his things and walked inside past a sign that read 'Sindertown Annual Art Exhibition'.

"Hello," a receptionist greeted him. "Are you here as an artist?" she asked politely.

"Yes I am!" Alex said joyfully.

"Excellent. Let's get you set up. Just head down that hall and take a right when you see signs for exhibition spots. From there show them your reservation and they will get you set up," she explained.

"Alright! Thank you," Alex replied as he headed that way.

After getting set up he waited with excitement as people started to admire his work.

"This one is really nice."

"I love the textures on this one."

"Woah, mommy look at this one!"

Compliments came as he told the people more about the pieces and handed out business cards where he could. Eventually a man in a suit and tie stopped and looked at his pieces.

"Hmm," the man said as he eyed the paintings. He was a very short man with a thin black hair that was starting to bald. "You seem to have very different styles or work from painting to painting."

"Yes sir," Alex replied half excited, half seriously. "I pride myself on being very versatile. No one style is good at getting every message across."

"I see," the man replied in a very gray tone. "You have talent. My name is Frank Walter," the man extended a hand to shake. "I'm looking for a strong artist to make original paintings for our company. I work for an interior decorating company. Would you mind if I took some snap shots to show my boss?" the man asked.

"No not at all," Alex said with a smile. "I also have plenty of cards if you would like to take a couple."

"Thank you," Frank replied as he accepted the cards.

After taking the pictures Frank shook Alex's hand again. "Thank you again. I look forward to seeing you again. You should hear something from me soon."

"Thank you. I look forward to hearing from you," Alex replied.

The man left, and the day continued. Alex talked and showed off his art to a huge audience as people came and went.

As Alex packed his things up into his car later that evening he looked up at the sky as the wind blew. With a smile on his face he closed the car door and let out a sigh of relief.

Chapter 13

Kelsey woke up around 9:30 and laid bed for a while. She looked at her phone and after pausing for a second put it back on her nightstand. She got comfortable and just as she closed her eyes a knock came at her door.

"Hey! I know you're up! You want to go to the fall festival with me?" Ashley asked through the door.

Kelsey stared at the door in silence with a slight look of fear in her eyes before slowly closing her eyes and getting comfortable again.

"You're not going back to sleep!" Ashley continued. "I'm gonna go get breakfast. Bye."

As Ashley started to walk away Kelsey called to her. "Bring me some coffee and a sandwich or something!"

"Only if you're up and getting ready," Ashley laughed and left to get food.

Kelsey laid back down and sighed.

"I guess it's my only day off work and school, I'd better enjoy it," she said to herself as she got up and showered.

After getting out she put on a pair of jeans and a tee shirt. Ashley was in the kitchen unpacking breakfast.

"You're wearing sweat pants and an old tee shirt!" Kelsey said as she walked in the kitchen. "You rushed me out of bed and you hadn't even started getting ready!" Irritation was subtle but real in her protests.

Ashley laughed. "I didn't say you had to be all the way done by the time I got back."

"I could have been sleeping for the next two hours while you get ready," Kelsey said dryly as she investigated her food. "You got me French toast!" she said with excitement, changing her mood entirely. "Aww! I only hate you a little bit for waking me up now," she said with a smile.

"Yea, you're welcome," Ashley said with a smirk and some sarcasm. "Besides, I don't take that long. I'll probably just shower and throw something on like you," she explained.

"What's that supposed to mean?" Kelsey asked. "I thought this was a cute shirt."

"It is," Ashley assured her. "I was just saying I won't worry about all the details and it'll be fast."

"I swear you're calling me ugly," Kelsey said as she cut her eyes at Ashley.

"I'm not!" Ashley defended with a laugh.

Kelsey laughed. "Go hurry up. It will be night time by the time you're ready."

"You're being dramatic," Ashley replied as she rolled her eyes.

An hour and half passed, and they were heading for the door to leave.

"I'm gonna get ready fast today," Kelsey laughed. "The worst part is this is actually faster than usual.

"I can't help it if my hair takes forever to straighten and the outfits I thought would look good didn't." Ashley defended.

"sure," Kelsey said. "I'm just ready to eat some funnel cake."

"Didn't you just eat some French toast?" Ashley asked.

"Yea three hours ago, when you started to get ready," Kelsey said.

"You're gonna get fat if you keep it up with these sweets," Ashley laughed.

"Good. Then I don't have to worry about impressing any guys and can live with my cats in peace," Kelsey explained calmly.

"You better stop!" Ashley laughed. "That might actually happen."

"I don't think you understand how serious I am," Kelsey replied dryly.

"Shut up," Ashley laughed. "I am jealous though," she continued as they got in the car to leave. "You can eat whatever you want and don't get any bigger. I even sniff a cupcake and I shoot up to 170."

"You're fine," Kelsey assured her dryly. "At least you have those monsters going for you," she laughed as she poked Ashley's chest.

"Stop it!" Ashley laughed as she pushed her away. "I'm gonna wreck. Are you trying to kill us?"

"I would never," Kelsey said innocently. "Spiked punch works much better," she added in a low tone with a mean smile.

Ashley looked at her seriously. "You're really creepy when you do that," she smiled. "You watch too many killer shows."

"How else am I supposed to get away with it when the time comes?" Kelsey laughed.

"You just don't do it!" Ashley said.

They both laughed as they headed to the fall festival.

Chapter 14

Ryan and Lindsey sat drinking coffee and talking on a bench at the park. It was mid-day and people were playing, walking their dogs, and jogging. The air was crisp and slightly chilly, so most people were wearing at least two layers.

"So tell me more about you," Lindsey said with a smile.

"Not much to say really," Ryan answered. "I'm pretty boring. Work all week, party on the weekend when I can."

"Oh come on!" Lindsey argued playfully. "You have to have more to you than that. You seem caring and kind of different. Where did you learn all that stuff about the stars? Or was that just a pick-up line?"

"No, it was really what I learned," Ryan replied. "I just look at them and read stuff about them sometimes. I just like how beautiful and big the night sky looks I guess. It's gay I know," he added with a half laugh.

"Oh my gosh! It's not gay," she argued. "I think it's cute."

"Yea," Ryan said dryly. "Cute."

"What's wrong with that?" Lindsey asked.

"Something about being a man and being cute don't mix with me," Ryan explained.

"Oh whatever," she said. "That's just what grizzly old angry men say. I'll bet it's girly to not have a beard too isn't it?"

"Trust me," Ryan said with a sigh, "I'm working on it. It just doesn't fill in and looks nasty."

"Please don't! I might have to stop talking to you," Lindsey laughed.

"You wouldn't," Ryan laughed.

"I don't know. It's getting cold outside, why don't you grow one and find out Mr. Mountain Man," she challenged him with a smile.

"What about you miss sass?" Ryan joked back. "What makes you tick?"

"Lots of coffee and a dark sense of humor," Lindsey laughed.

Ryan chuckled. "There has to be more than that?" he asked with genuine concern.

Lindsey paused. "Well I don't really know what to say. Most people don't just sit down and ask you about your entire life. It's more 'Hey how ya been? Work? Kids? Good. Good. Good. Bye.'"

"That's about all people really have," Ryan said.

"There's more, there has to be," Lindsey said.

"Then where's yours?" Ryan laughed.

"Hey, I asked you first!" Lindsey protested.

"Not so easy, is it?" Ryan challenged.

"You'll be ok," Lindsey said with a smile.

Ryan leaned back and sighed, smiling and shaking his head, "You're something else I swear," he said.

"I'm not so bad once you get to know me," she smiled confidently at him.

"If I make it that long," Ryan smiled.

"What's that supposed to mean?" she asked.

"Oh nothing, you're not crazy I promise," Ryan said seriously with a smile after.

"You think I'm crazy?" Lindsey asked with a serious frown.

"Hey, I was just joking. Don't be sad," Ryan reassured her seriously.

Lindsey smiled. "Oh yea, you're not going anywhere."

"Hey! I felt bad for that. You can't mess with me like that," Ryan said.

"I was just kidding. I'm actually really sweet like an angel," she explained with an innocent smile.

"I'm starting to think you might be part monster," Ryan said with a smile as he eyed her cautiously.

"You'll have to wait and see," Lindsey said with a smile.

"Are you gonna be off next Saturday?" Ryan asked.

"Yea I should be, what's up?"

"Wanna go to the fall festival with me?"

"Sounds like fun!"

"Ok cool!"

She looked at him for a second. Responding to this Ryan's cheeks turned slightly red.

"You're adorable sometimes," Lindsey said with a smile.

"Hey now, easy with all that," Ryan said. "We've been through this. Cute, adorable, sweet, none of these are acceptable ways to describe a man."

"Then I guess you're still a boy," Lindsey said and started laughing.

"Oh my gosh," Ryan sighed and smiled. "I'm taking it back. No fall festival for you."

"But..." she replied as her face sunk.

"Nope, not gonna work," Ryan said seriously.

"It's ok," Lindsey smiled. "I'll see you Saturday."

Chapter 15

Gerome got off work almost an hour after he normally did and headed to his car.

"See you next week," he said dryly to himself.

Gerome arrived back at his apartment and kicked off his shoes before falling on his couch. After an exhausted sigh, he laid there for minutes with his eyes closed. He fell asleep for almost twenty minutes before jumping awake.

"Shit," he said as he checked his phone for the time. He closed his eyes again. "Ugh, I'm like some old man already."

He looked at his phone one more time before deciding to get up and get ready to go out.

Gerome walked into the pizza place and was greeted with the smell of fresh pizza, fried wings, and a hint of cheap beer. The place was busy but not packed, people ate, laughed, talked, and walked outside to smoke.

"Hey!" the hostess greeted him. "Are you eating at the bar or a table?"

"The bar should be fine. Thank you," he replied with a smile.

"Ok," she said cheerfully and went back to folding silverware in napkins.

Gerome made his way to the bar and sat.

"What can I get you?" the bartender asked.

"Just some water and a menu for now," he replied.

"Ok not a problem," she answered.

Gerome eyed the menu for a long time looking back and forth at the choices.

"Do you have slices?" he asked the bartender.

"Sorry Hun, we only sell them at lunch," she informed him.

"Ok, that's fine," he replied as he looked at the menu again.

"Hey Rachel!" Demetry called as he turned the corner to the bar area. "Order 57... Dude! G you showed up!" he said as he saw Gerome.

"What's up man," Gerome replied with a smile.

"What about 57?" Rachel asked.

"Oh," Demetry said getting back on track. "Just find out what kind of sauce they want with their wings."

"I think it was ranch," she said.

"Ok cool," he said and then turned to Gerome again. "Dude what are you drinking tonight? Next one's on me."

"Just water," Gerome chuckled.

"You don't come out on Friday night to hang out and not have a single drink," Demetry protested. "Rachel get this a double shot of firestorm." He leaned in close to Rachel and smiled. "And one for me too."

"I'll put it on your tab," Rachel smiled as she poured the shots.

"Sweet," Demetry replied.

Rachel put the shots on the bar.

"I don't know man," Gerome half laughed.

"Go! Go!" Demetry said with a slick look left and right scanning the bar. He grabbed his shot and tapped it on the bar.

With no time to react Gerome grabbed his shot and quickly tapped it on the bar before taking it.

With a sharp exhale and a few coughs Gerome recovered from the drink. "Holy cow, that's stronger than I remember."

"You're out of the game man!" Demetry laughed. "I gotta run back to work before this place burns down. He motioned Gerome for a fist bump. "Rachel any drink this man wants gets put on my tab tonight," he said as the two men fist bumped.

"Thanks man," Gerome said as Demetry left back to work.

"No problem!" Demetry called back. "I'll tell the guys you're here."

"So, you're the G everybody talks about," Rachel smiled.

Gerome smiled. "I guess I am," he said as he shrugged his shoulders.

"It's funny you don't look anything like I would have imagined," Rachel noted. "But not in a bad way," she quickly added.

"Yea," Gerome said. "A lot has changed."

"I'll bet a lot has stayed the same too," Rachel added.

"What do you mean?" Gerome asked.

"I don't think people change," she explained. "They get older, change jobs, move away, have kids, settle down, but deep down I think they stay the same on the inside."

"Maybe," Gerome said. "I never really thought about stuff like that I guess."

Rachel half laughed. "I think about stuff like that too much. So, you know what you want yet?" she asked.

"Let me just get a small pie with onions, peppers, mushrooms please, and a PDR," he added.

"On tap or can?" she asked.

"On tap is fine," Gerome replied. "Also put this on my own tab," he smiled, "but don't tell D."

"You got it," she winked at him.

After a while his food came out being held by a towering man sporting a full beard and a body full of tattoos.

"Digs!" Gerome said with excitement.

"Is that really you?" Digs asked in his deep voice. "What are you wearing? Where's your hair?" he asked as he sat the food on the counter and looked for a hug.

Gerome stood up and Digs squeezed him as he tried to reply. "It's just a golf shirt and shorts," he defended as he hugged back. "It's regular causal wear."

The two stepped back from each other.

"D was right…" Digs said with a serious tone. "You really have been brainwashed."

"I'm not brainwashed," Gerome laughed. "This is just what they wear in the business world so it's all I have. It was this or the monkey suit."

"We have a lot of catching up to do," Digs said. "We close in an hour or two, you gonna be here?"

"Yea I can stay, have a couple beers, hang out," Gerome said excitedly.

"All right!" Digs replied. "I'll make you some wings. You still like the lemon pepper?"

"That's fine, you don't have too..." Gerome started to say.

"10-4! Lemon pepper and the reaper sauce," Digs said quickly as he walked back to the kitchen.

"These guys are too much," Gerome laughed as he sat back down. "Hey Rachel, can I have another PDR?"

"Sure thing," she replied with a smile.

Gerome drank and ate until they closed, talking to Rachel and other bar goers. The guys came to the bar once the kitchen was closed.

"Those wings were killer Digs, thanks man," Gerome said as he finished off the last of his beer.

"Yea! Time for a shot!" Demetry said as he poured shots for everyone. The only ones left in the restaurant were Demetry, Digs, Gerome, Rachel, and Paul.

Paul was average height and very skinny. He had pale skin and long straight black hair down to the middle of his back.

They all held their glasses up and tapped them on the bar before taking the shots.

"How you been Paul?" Gerome asked after he finished his shot.

Paul just smiled and replied in his quiet voice. "Pretty good man, just enjoying every day as it comes."

"Hell yea!" Gerome replied. He leaned back in his chair and exhaled. "This is nice."

"You seem like you haven't been able to relax in a while," Digs noted.

"Yea man, work has been killer lately, but I'm close to a promotion. It's gonna be nice, less grunt work and more money," Gerome explained.

"I'll bet those stuff shirts can't hang anyway," Demetry laughed.

"You'd be surprised," Gerome said seriously. "Last summer party some people got a little to... friendly, with their bottles."

"Dang man, you're rich, famous, getting promotions, summer parties, you've got it all," Demetry laughed.

"Yea right," Gerome laughed. "It's not that nice, but it has its moments."

"I guess were never getting you back in the band, are we?" Digs asked with a smile.

"I'm old and boring now," Gerome explained with a laugh. "You don't want me. By the way, who is this new guy?"

"He's a total tool," Demetry said. "Dude can shred, but He's got no respect and no manners. He's slowly giving us a bad name. He sprays beer on the crowd, talks shit to the fans, refuses to sign merch."

"He can be pretty unpleasant," Paul added.

"Damn, if Paul doesn't like him, something is really wrong," Gerome laughed.

"Yea," Digs sighed. "Were just in a bad spot. We have shows booked but with no Albus, no shows."

"His name is Albus?" Gerome asked.

"Yea," Digs replied.

"Sounds like a tool name!" Gerome laughed, and the others joined in. "So how did you manage to get this set-up? You guys just run the place?"

"Many years of weeding out the bad ones and hiring our friends," Demetry laughed. "But we don't run anything, just really close to the owner, he trusts us."

"Dang that's pretty sick," Gerome replied then yawned. "Man, what time is it?"

"Almost twelve," Digs replied.

"That's a lot later than I'm usually up," Gerome laughed. "I'm normally passed out by ten."

"You gotta spend more time with us," Demetry insisted. "Loosen up before you really become a stuff shirt business man."

Gerome laughed. "Maybe you're right, but not every weekend. I need to find sleep somewhere."

"Speaking of every weekend, are you free next Saturday?" Digs asked.

"I should be," Gerome replied.

"Were all gonna head to the fall festival if you want to come?" Digs offered.

"I should be able to do that," Gerome said.

"Sweet!" Demetry said. "It'll be just like old times... only without the whole punk spraying graffiti thing," he laughed.

"Yea," Gerome laughed. "I can't go to jail again. They let you off easy when you're a kid." He stood up and stretched.

"Alright man," Digs said. "It was good catching up."

"Drive safe," Demetry said.

"See you next weekend," Paul said.

"Nice meeting you," Rachel said from down the bar where she was putting cups away.

"You too!" Gerome called back. "See you guys," he waved as he walked out the front door.

Chapter 16

It was mid-day at The Coffee Hole and people were bustling back and forth, or sitting down enjoying lunch. Alex was talking to a girl at one of the tables.

"It's so awesome!" Alex explained." I'm just waiting for a reply and I could have a huge thing going for me."

"That's so cool. I'm glad your career is really blowing up, you're really talented," she encouraged him. "Me and Brandon are still saving for a place," she sounded disappointed.

"It will come, trust me!" Alex said with a smile. "If you just keep your head up and move forward everything will work out, I promise. It's easier said than done, I know, but think about every other time you had to wait for something. It came to you just in time, didn't it?"

"Yea," she chuckled. "You're very right on that one. I love catching you from time to time, you always bring happiness wherever you go. You're so inspirational."

"The world needs all it can get," Alex said happily. "That's why they need more paintings to make them happy… and make me filthy rich!" he laughed.

"You probably wouldn't even spend it on a big house or car if you had it," she joked.

"Not on me," Alex laughed. "But plenty of other people would have blessings sent to them left and right."

The young lady finished her coffee and stood up. "Well I'm back to class," she said.

"Ok have fun!" Alex said.

"Yea right," she rolled her eyes.

"Don't forget to come support your favorite artist at the fall festival this Saturday," Alex added.

"Ok!" she smiled and left.

Tom walked up to the table.

"Do you know everyone?" he asked.

"Nah," Alex laughed, "just most of them. It's because I'm friendly. You should try it sometime," he joked.

"You're a hippie who loiters around my shop every day harassing my customers," Tom said dryly.

"Oh come on! Just because I'm a white guy with dreads doesn't mean I'm a hippie. I just want to be an artist, and they say you need to dress the part if you want the job," he laughed.

"Peace and love brother," Tom said with two fingers held up in a peace sign.

"Dude! Our minds are just electricity. Does that mean that thunder clouds are just giant air brains that could even be smarter than us?" Alex asked in a slow tone while keeping his eyes half open.

"Don't ever do that again," Tom said seriously. "You'll scare away all my customers and turn this place into some hipster paradise."

Alex laughed. "Yea that would be bad."

"You still living with that roommate over by the mall?" Tom asked.

"Yea same place," Alex answered.

"He still having grandma pay all the bills while you... dare I say, work for a living?" Tom asked.

Alex laughed. "He's not so bad. I don't think sitting around all day smoking weed is the ideal life, but he seems... happy."

"I say you get out of that place," Tom warned. "He's trouble and He's only going to bring you down."

"Soon I'll be able to do whatever I want," Alex explained. "I've got a big deal with a company downtown and I'm going to have a 'real job'."

"Real job? Doing what?" Tom asked.

"Painting for an interior decorating company," Alex informed him.

"Hmm," Tom replied.

"What?" Alex asked.

"Nothing, just couldn't see you in a suit, taking orders and painting what they tell you when they tell you," Tom explained.

"It won't be like that," Alex protested. "They liked my art and chose me. I doubt they will just tell me to do something totally opposite of what they liked in the first place."

"You might be right," Tom said.

"You're gonna be dying for my paintings when I'm the artist who makes the paintings in five-star hotels," Alex bragged. "And it will be too late, you had your chance."

"I doubt that," Tom laughed. "Stay out of trouble," he said as he went to tend to the store.

"Yes sir!" Alex replied with a military salute.

Chapter 17

The fall festival was in full swing Saturday. Half the city had traffic blocked off and events were set up everywhere. A tasty aroma filled the air on west main street, the smell from all the food trucks melted together. Live bands of all kinds were scattered throughout the streets. Vendors and street performers smiled and talked to the hundreds of people walking. Children played with their new toys, running around with leaves and pumpkins painted on their faces.

Kelsey and Ashley were walking down the street while Kelsey enjoyed a big plate filled with funnel cake.

"What do you want to do next little piggy?" Ashley joked.

"Mehhouh ummbbb bahmm…" Kelsey started to say with a mouth full.

Ashley burst out laughing "Blub blub blub blub!" she mocked with puffed out cheeks.

Kelsey swallowed the food and laughed. "Leave me alone! This is delicious, and I don't really care." They walked for a moment. "Wanna visit the shops?"

"Yea, let's do it," Ashley agreed. "We can take that cool train thing! I think it starts down the road."

The girls waited for their ride. While they waited a group of people walked up behind them. They talked amongst themselves and waited as well. After a moment Kelsey turned around. Gerome, Digs, Demetry, Rachel, and Paul were standing behind them waiting.

"Oh! Mr. Melton," she said as she seen Gerome. "I thought I heard a familiar voice."

"Oh hey," Gerome replied cheerfully.

"Mr. Melton!" Digs joked. "You really got a pretty big name for yourself!"

Gerome sighed. "You can just call me Gerome," he said with a laugh.

"Ok," Kelsey said with a smile.

"Katie, right?" Gerome asked.

"Kelsey," she corrected.

"Sorry…" Gerome apologized.

"Come on man!" Demetry said. "You can't even remember this beautiful girl's name after she calls you Mr. Melton?"

"Come on guys, cut me some slack here," Gerome pleaded.

"It's ok," Kelsey said with a laugh. "I'm just good with names."

"Who are your friends?" Ashley asked.

"Gerome comes to the shop all the time," Kelsey explained. "I don't think I've met you guys though?" she asked the rest of the group.

"These are my friends from high school," Gerome said.

"I guess were not friends anymore," Digs said.

"You know what I meant!" Gerome defended himself. "This is Digs, Demetry, Paul, and Rachel."

"Nice to meet you," Kelsey greeted.

"So what are you guys up to?" Gerome asked Kelsey.

"Going to look at some shops," she replied. "You?"

"Same," Gerome said. "I gotta find some stuff to decorate my apartment. It's felt like some bland cardboard box for a while."

"I don't even know what I want," Kelsey explained. "Nothing honestly, but I'm here so I figure why not try to have some fun."

"Yea, the guys asked me to come out, so I figured why not," Gerome replied.

"I was kidnapped and forced by my roommate," Kelsey laughed.

"Man, that's harsh," Gerome replied.

"First you don't introduce me, then you call me a kidnapper," Ashley protested.

"Oh my god, I'm so sorry," Kelsey said with wide eyes. "This is Ashley, she's my roommate."

"Nice to meet you"

"Hey"

"Don't worry it's happened to me"

The group greeted her.

Kelsey laughed. "She's really not that bad," she said to Gerome. "If I didn't have her I probably would never see the light of day again. Just hiding in my room under fifteen blankets, I'd slowly fade away."

Gerome laughed. "I could probably say the same, but my home life doesn't seem nearly as appealing as yours."

"It's all about the blankets and pillows," Kelsey explained. "You need the right balance of comfort and ease of access. Too many and you can't function, too little and you're not snug. Then you have your snacks and show line up." She gave him a serious look. "There is a long list of things to getting the perfect set up."

"Shit," Gerome said.

"I think I need to be taking notes," Digs laughed.

The train pulled up and they all shuffled on board. Kelsey looked towards the back, waved and smiled before sitting down.

"Who's that?" Lindsey asked.

"She's a girl I know from The Coffee Hole, she usually works when I get my morning coffee," Ryan explained.

"Oh, are you guys friends?" Lindsey asked.

"Not really friends, but I've talked to her a couple of times about work and stuff, nothing serious," Ryan said downplaying the situation.

"Well let's say hey. She must think you're a friend to wave. And look, they are all together, maybe they are doing something fun," she insisted.

"I guess," Ryan said hesitantly.

"You are the life of the party, Mr. Social, when you're drunk. What's wrong now?" Lindsey asked playfully.

"I don't know," he said. "I guess I just didn't want to go getting excited about some other girl when we are here together," Ryan explained.

"That's different if were on a romantic, personal date, like when we had dinner and laid out under the stars," she replied.

The two made their way up a couple of seats.

"Hey Kelsey," Ryan said. "What are you guys up too?"

"Going to the shops to buy things we don't actually need and never use them," Kelsey laughed. "Is this your girlfriend?"

"Yea, this is Lindsey," Ryan said.

"Hey," Lindsey greeted them with a smile.

Ashley and Kelsey were sitting in the seats in front of them with Paul and Rachel across the aisle, and Digs in front of them, while Demetry and Gerome sat in front of Kelsey and Ashley.

"Got room for two more in your group?" Lindsey asked.

"I don't see why not," Kelsey laughed. "I actually just met half of them a couple of minutes ago."

Kelsey introduced everyone and they all got to say hey just as the train stopped.

Everyone shuffled off the train slowly. Once they were all off Demetry asked Gerome.

"Where to captain?"

"What do you mean captain?" Gerome asked.

"You're the one who needs furniture," Demetry laughed.

"Not furniture," Gerome laughed. "Just stuff to make the place feel more like home."

"We should check out that tent," Ashley said. "It looks like they might have some cool stuff."

"It's decided," Digs said. "To the tent."

They all looked around for a while and Rachel ended up buying a dream catcher.

"I want to try and get some pictures," Gerome said. "My walls are kinda bare."

"I think I seen a place that had some paintings down the road," Demetry replied.

They walked down the road to the place and Alex was sitting in a chair next to paintings he had on display.

"It's you!" Gerome said.

"Heyyy! It's the bowl of fruit guy," Alex replied with a smile.

"Hey Alex," Kelsey said.

"Hey kels," Alex replied. "It's crazy, you two know each other?"

"We have all actually met at The Coffee Hole," Kelsey explained. "You have probably seen each other once or twice."

"Hold on!" Alex stopped. "Are you guys part of Trailing the Light?"

"Yea!" Demetry replied excitedly. "You've heard of us?"

"Yea, I seen one of your shows a while back at Shred Cavern and actually picked up an album. You're really good," Alex complimented.

"Damn," Ryan chuckled. "I built that place."

"No way!" Demetry asked. "You built the Shred Cavern?"

"Not all of it," Ryan laughed. "Back then I was more of a helper than a builder actually. One thing I can take credit for is screwing up the east side bathroom. That entire wall is completely off level and not parallel to the rest of the building."

"I told you!" Demetry shouted to Digs. "I knew there was something wrong with that room!"

"What?" Ryan asked.

"We all call that the ghost room, because everybody knows something is wrong, but nobody knew what it was," Demetry explained.

"Yea, that was pretty much my fault. The project was rushed also, that didn't help," Ryan replied.

"I never noticed it," Digs said. "I just thought he was crazy. Now I'm never gona hear the end of it." He laughed.

"So did you come for a painting or just to say hey?" Alex asked cheerfully.

"I still need a painting," Gerome laughed.

"Well what do you want?" Alex asked him.

"This one looks nice," Gerome said as he looked at the selection.

"No way," Alex said. "You can't have those. You were supposed to find yourself remember."

"Oh come on," Gerome laughed.

"I'm serious," Alex smiled.

The others looked at paintings and talked amongst themselves.

"Maybe the ocean," Gerome offered.

"Maybe," Alex said.

"I just want to have a picture in my living room!" Gerome pleaded.

"I know," Alex laughed. "You just have to find out what you really want."

"I don't understand you," Gerome said as he half laughed half sighed.

"I think he's on to something," Demetry said. "You can spend money on a big picture and it not be the right one."

"Not you too…" Gerome sighed.

"Think about it, a man can't just put random stuff in their house that they don't even really like," Demetry reasoned.

"See! He understands," Alex agreed.

"I like the ocean!" Gerome protested. "I'm just gonna go home and throw paint all over the walls," he said with a sarcastic but happy tone.

"Now were talking!" Alex said happily.

The three of them laughed.

"Hey guys," Kelsey said. "We're gonna go grab a drink. If we don't make it back before you leave, it was nice seeing you."

"Well hey if everybody is off why don't we all do what we need to and then hang out tonight?" Demetry suggested. "Poor Paul and Rachel have to work, but the rest of us are off. We could get some food."

"That sounds like fun," Lindsey said. "What do you think babe?" she asked Ryan.

"Sure, I don't mind," Ryan replied.

"I don't go back to work till Monday, so why not," Gerome said.

"What do you think?" Kelsey asked Ashley.

"I actually have plans with friends," Ashley informed her.

"Ok, that's fine," Kelsey said. "I have to work tomorrow in the morning, so I don't think I can tonight."

"Oh come on," Demetry said. "We won't be out late."

"Come on guys. Do you know how much it took to even do this? I might die if I try for any more social interaction," Kelsey pleaded jokingly.

"You don't even have any projects this weekend," Ashley noted. "This is the perfect time."

Kelsey sat quiet for a second. "Ok, fine."

"Yea!" the group cheered.

"But only till eight or so!" Kelsey added.

"Sounds good to me!" Gerome said.

"And you?" Demetry asked Alex.

"Heck yea! Why not?" Alex said.

"Sweet. Wanna meet at the big water fountain around six?" Demetry asked.

"That's fine."

"Yea, sure."

"I can do that."

"No problem."

"Sweet I guess we'll see you there," Demetry said as he waved to Kelsey and Ashley as they left.

"Ok," Kelsey replied.

"Bye everyone! Nice to meet you," Ashley called.

"Bye you too!" the group called back.

"I guess we're gonna go try and find some more furniture since he can't have a painting yet," Demetry laughed.

"Alright man," Alex replied.

"See you guys," Ryan said.

"Bye," Lindsey said.

"And what can I do for you nice folks?" Alex asked Ryan and Lindsey after the others left.

"I like this painting," Ryan said as he looked at a painting of a forest at night. The forest had a glow from the inside the trees. The glow was greenish blue in the dark blue and black of the forest. Above the forest was a huge expanse of stars covering the forest almost like a blanket.

"Ahh," Alex said. "This one is very peaceful. It's strange how it seems so dark, but the longer you look at, the more it seems to glow."

"How much is it?" Ryan asked.

"It's seventy-five," Alex informed them. "But I can see the look in your eyes, it tells me this painting was made for you. I can do fifty."

"Are you sure?" Ryan asked.

"Yea," Alex said. "To see someone who really appreciates my work and find the true home for a painting is what I live for."

"Thanks man," Ryan replied. "I really do like it. I'll tell you what, sixty and I'll buy you a beer tonight. How's that sound?"

"Sounds good to me," Alex said happily.

The two men shook on it and Ryan and Lindsey left.

Chapter 18

It was 5:45 and Kelsey sat on a bench next to the water fountain. Gerome walked up and sat with her.

"Hey," he greeted her. "Nobody here yet?"

"Nah, not yet," she replied.

"This is pretty weird," Gerome said as he looked off into the distance. "I didn't really see anyone outside of work for almost a year. Just work, home, repeat. Maybe going out once every couple of months. It's like I'm living a new life all of a sudden."

"Yea, I guess I can say the same," Kelsey replied. "I see a lot of people at work and school, but nothing really meaningful. This is one of the first times in a while that

I've actually been out like this. Not sure if it's good or bad," she laughed.

"I feel like I needed it," Gerome said. "I spent so much energy on my job. I needed a break. Now I need to be careful though. Partying and hanging out is nice, but I can't let it get in the way of my job."

"Yea, moments where I can relax really make me just want to quit school and work and just live in my bed," Kelsey laughed.

"You're going for nursing, right?" Gerome asked.

"Yea," Kelsey replied.

"That must be rough. Not many people can do it I feel like," Gerome said.

"I don't even think I can do it," Kelsey explained. "I just want to help people," she explained. "Being able to help save lives, but more than that, it's the daily things. I'm not going to the doctor doing the real saving, but I get to be the face that sees the patients all the time. I get to laugh with them and them stories to cheer them up even during the worst of times. At least that's the nurses I remember when I was a kid."

"Man, that's really cool," Gerome said quietly.

"Sorry," Kelsey said with a half laugh.

"You're fine," Gerome assured her. "That is really cool. Don't give up."

"Thanks," she replied. "What made you so passionate about business?"

"I guess I just don't want to feel like I wasted my life," he explained. "You have to work in this world if you want to make it. Sitting on your ass will never get you ahead. I want a nice life. I want a nice car, nice house, nice job, money, respect, and this is how you get all of those."

"Yea, I guess you're right about that," Kelsey noted.

"Right about what?" Alex asked from behind them with a smile.

Kelsey jumped slightly, and Gerome turned.

"Talking about how we have to work through school and a job to make it," Gerome laughed. "Why can't we all just paint, or be actors, or be in a band!" he pointed at Digs and Demetry and said the last part louder.

"Are you kidding me? Do you have any idea how many classes I had to ignore to doddle all day in school? Having to tune out that teacher can be difficult, then you lose drawing time by getting sent to the office for 'disobedience'." He said the last part with finger quotes and a laugh.

Gerome and Kelsey laughed, and the two band members made it to the bench.

"What's up guys?" Demetry asked as he walked up.

"Sup man," Gerome replied.

"Just waiting on the builder?" Demetry asked.

"Yea, Ryan and his girlfriend," Kelsey explained. "I think he said her name was Lindsey."

"I swear I thought her name was Chelsea…" Gerome laughed. "You really saved me there."

"No problem," Kelsey smiled. "It's kinda part of my job to remember names."

"Hey, there he is," Digs pointed to the two as they approached.

"Sup," Ryan said.

"What's going on man?" Digs asked with a fist bump.

"Now that we all made it, where do we eat?" Demetry asked.

"I'm part garbage disposal, I'll eat anything," Ryan said. "Plus, I don't want any part of this debate," he laughed.

"Hell yea, I can dig that," Digs replied.

"Oh really? Can you… dig… that?" Demetry asked.

"Oh god…" Digs sighed and shook his head.

Half the crowd started laughing and the others looked confused.

"Oh come on! Dig? Digs! That's gold!" Demetry protested.

"Ohh! I get it!" Alex started laughing.

Lindsey's eyes widened a bit and she started laughing

"See! They just didn't remember your name," Demetry laughed.

"Either way, I don't care where we eat," Digs said with a smile.

"As long as it's not spicy I don't really care," Gerome said.

"I just don't want to eat pizza," Lindsey said. "I've had way too much recently."

"I know the feeling," Digs said.

"I'm ok for anything," Kelsey said.

"We can try that all you can eat place down the road," Alex suggested.

"Oh hell yea!" Digs said.

"All you can eat anything is always a good call," Ryan added.

"This man gets it," Digs said.

"I'm cool with that," Demetry said.

"That's fine," Kelsey said.

"Same," Lindsey agreed.

"I can do that," Gerome said.

"Sweet, I really wanted some sushi," Alex laughed.

"Enjoy all you want," Ryan laughed. "I'm not eating that crap."

"I thought you were part garbage disposal?" Alex joked.

"Yea for real food," Ryan explained. "That's got a chance to poison you, it's not even cooked."

"I like the cooked kind," Kelsey added as they walked to the restaurant.

"I didn't even know they made cooked sushi," Lindsey said. "What do they do just fry em' or boil em'?"

"I guess it's however you want it," Kelsey replied.

"Wouldn't the rice burn if you grilled it?" Lindsey asked.

"You don't cook the whole thing," Kelsey laughed. "Just the fish before you make it."

The whole group laughed.

"I don't know how they make sushi!" Lindsey laughed.

"It's ok," Ryan laughed. "I just pictured them deep frying the whole thing when she said that."

"That actually sounds pretty good," Demetry said. "I think it would work."

"You can deep fry anything if you put your mind to it," Kelsey explained. "You should see the deep-frying competitions they have."

"Wait people have deep-frying competitions?" Gerome asked.

"You'd be surprised at what people do when you follow the video hole deep enough online," Kelsey said seriously.

The rest of them laughed and they made their way to the restaurant.

They all found seats and went to get food when they arrived at the restaurant. Most of them came back with a plate that had a mixture of everything on it. Alex returned with a mountain of sushi and Digs ended up with three plates piled high with food before he sat down.

"Holy crap," Lindsey said. "You hungry?" she asked Digs.

"Way I see it, you're gonna make three trips or more anyway. I want to sit down and enjoy my food without having to run around in between plates," he explained.

"That's true," Gerome said. "But what if you don't know what you want or get full?"

"If you get full after round one or two you don't deserve the buffet life," Digs laughed.

"This guy is pretty smart," Ryan chuckled to Lindsey.

"I do what I can," Digs said with a smile.

The conversations evolved separately as they all talked amongst themselves.

"It's so crazy to just be hanging out having dinner with you guys. I've listened to your music a lot," Alex said to Demetry.

"Thanks man, it means a lot. All we really hope for is to make good sound for people to enjoy. It's probably the same for your art," Demetry said.

"Yea, it's nice to know that my paintings will make someone happy for years tome come when they see them," Alex noted.

"Yea, and one thing we can do as artists is give people a place to turn to. Sometimes people need inspiration, comfort, or just something they can relax too. When you hear a song, or see a picture that really lifts you up, it can be the difference in your whole day," Demetry said seriously.

"You're exactly right," Alex replied. "I think that's why we are so important to the world. We can capture emotion and put it into a medium that other people can use to make their lives better."

"Not just that either," Demetry said. "At least I know with music we can make songs that let people know they are not alone. The world can get you down sometimes. It makes you feel so beaten down and alone, like nobody understands. We can speak to people. We can let them know that it's not just them. We all face these problems."

"I feel like sad paintings will make people sad," Alex said. "I don't want my art to bring people down."

"They do," Demetry replied, but just like a sad song they are necessary. They allow people to let out the sadness inside them. People don't like to face their problems. They hide from them and cover them up with anger or other things, but they can cry at a sad song or movie. They don't know it, but they are letting out some of their own tears in there as well."

"You think so?"

"Maybe, who knows, I'd like to think it has to be something."

"So you know how to build things?" Digs asked Ryan.

"Yea," Ryan replied. "Been doing it since I was sixteen or so."

"Dang, rough life," Digs replied.

"It's not so bad one you get used to it. It's pretty much all I know. My dad is actually the boss, so he's the real reason I got this far. Taught me everything I know," Ryan explained.

"That's pretty cool. I still can't believe you helped build Shred Cavern," Digs said.

"Yea, that's the best part about the job," Ryan explained. "Some days suck, but once it's over and I see all of the people enjoying the buildings I built, that's a good feeling."

"Dang, I never thought about it that way," Digs said. "That sounds really cool."

"That's because I'm talking about it," Ryan laughed. "On any given day I hate that job. I hate the hours, the work, the freezing cold, the insane heat, it all sucks. I just remember my friends and all the fun times we had building, and it sounds better than it is."

"Man don't ruin it for me now!" Digs laughed. "I was about to quit the pizza business and go join you."

"Please don't," Ryan laughed. After a pause he continued, "I'll bet it's nice being in a band. You get to do what you love every day."

"That's what you'd think," Digs warned. "It's nice most days, but it can be stressful. You have to practice the same song over, and over, and over and then play it for shows after that. It makes you almost get tired of it. Then there is the fact that we are still not big enough to live off the music, so we have to stick at this restaurant. It's not a bad job by any means, but it can be a lot to work all day, then try to play a show, then back to work the next morning because some asshole called out. I guess it's like we need the job to support the band, but the job holds us back. Kinda shitty situation."

"I know what you're saying with people calling out," Ryan said sadly. "I've worked plenty of sixteen hour shifts because people can't just show up for work and we have a deadline to make."

"You play any instruments?" Digs asked.

"Nah," Ryan laughed. "I'd make better sound with nails on a chalk board."

Digs laughed. "Well what do you do to let off steam?"

"Party mostly," Ryan explained. "I've got her now too." He elbowed Lindsey. "She keeps me pretty busy, always trying to get me to try new things."

"Don't let him lie to you," Lindsey said. "He's an amateur astrologist."

"Dang really?" Digs asked. "That's pretty sick."

"I'm not even close," Ryan laughed. "I just like to look at them. Its relaxing."

"Well everybody has to have something," Digs said.

They all carried on conversations while they finished their food.

"Oh come on! Just a little bit!" Demetry insisted as he held a plate of wasabi to Gerome's face.

"Dude, you know I don't do spicy stuff," Gerome laughed.

"I'll do it if you do it," Lindsey challenged. "Come on Kelsey."

"Yea! Wasabi party!" Alex said as he held up a big portion on his chopsticks.

"Why not," Ryan laughed.

"If somebody brings me some I will," Digs laughed.

"You lazy..." Gerome started to say with a laugh.

"Don't worry, I've got plenty," Alex assured them.

The group of them took portions of wasabi.

"Cheers!" Demetry said and they all ate it.

"That's not so bad," Kelsey said right before putting her hand over her mouth. "oh!" she called out as her face turned red.

"What the hell!" Ryan said. "My nose."

All of them laughed at each other with watery eyes and red faces except Alex. After the heat had subsided they calmed down and got ready to leave.

"This was fun," Lindsey said cheerfully.

"Yea it was!" Demetry replied.

"It was pretty fun," Kelsey said with a smile. "Even though I stayed a bit later than I wanted to."

"We'll all have to hang out again when were free one night," Digs offered.

"For sure," Ryan said.

They made their way to the street after paying for dinner.

"We all got each others numbers, right?" Gerome asked.

"Yea, I think so," Demetry replied and looked around at everybody.

"Sweet, see you guys soon," Gerome said.

"Bye!" everyone said their goodbyes and went their separate ways.

Chapter 19

Ryan sat on a stack of bricks eating lunch with his co-workers at a job site. He was talking to Luis.

"So what's up with you and this girl?" Luis asked.

"What do you mean?" Ryan asked in return.

"You been spending a lot of time with her, seems like you don't even hang anymore," Luis told him.

"Nah, it's not like that," Ryan explained. "Just trying to find time for everything."

"Do you love her?" Luis asked with a concerned tone.

"Woah, I don't know about all that," Ryan said. "I do like her a lot. It's like she is something I never knew I needed."

"Oh yea, you love her," Luis said convincingly. "Don't worry, she ever breaks your heart, I know some fat bitches that will beat her ass for a sack of weed."

"I know," Ryan said seriously. "Thanks man."

"I got you homie," Luis said.

"So, you fuck her yet?" one of the guys asked as he tuned into their conversation.

"Come on eddy," Ryan laughed.

"I'm just asking!" Eddy defended with a smile.

"No, I didn't," Ryan answered.

"But you got some head?" Eddy asked.

"I don't wanna talk about this," Ryan laughed. "I actually like this girl."

"Ayy! He didn't deny it!" one of the other guys said.

"I knew it," Eddy said happily. "Was it good? Did she hit with her teeth?"

"A come on, leave him alone," a heavy-set Latino guy jumped in. "He's in love."

"Man, shut up Gordo," Eddy said. "What are you his psychologist?"

"You don't even know what that word means, dumbass," Gordo replied.

"Man, fuck you fatass," Eddy said back.

"Don't get mad at me because a fat dude pulls more bitches, and is smarter than you," Gordo countered with a smile.

"You don't even pull bitches though!" Eddy protested. "You just talk to them all night on some gay shit. You're not even fucking them."

"Bro! That's how you get them to come back," Gordo explained. "That's why you pull em for one night and I got a whole contact list full of bitches right now."

"Yea right," Eddy scoffed.

"Bet!" Gordo challenged as he hopped up and put his hand out. "Bet! I got fifty says I got more bitches that will reply if I message them right now."

The two carried on back and forth as lunch went on.

"So you hanging out with her again this weekend?" Luis asked Ryan.

"Yea, she said she has something special for me," Ryan explained.

"Ayy! Something special," Luis said with a sly grin.

"Yea, yea," Ryan said. "It's probably just some fancy date or something."

"Well best of luck bro," Luis said as he got up.

"Thanks man," Ryan replied.

Saturday night Lindsey picked Ryan up from his house and they left late in the evening.

"What are you up to?" Ryan asked with a smile.

"You'll just have to wait and see," Lindsey replied with a cheeky grin as they headed down the road.

"Whatever you say," he replied as he leaned back.

"I'm actually gonna need you to put this on, ok," she informed him as she handed him a folded-up bandana.

"Put this on?" Ryan asked. "For what?"

"So you don't ruin the surprise!" she insisted.

He laughed. "Ok, ok." After putting the blindfold on he said, "You're probably taking me to a dark place so you can kill me."

"Noooo…," she assured him. "… ok maybe," she added. "But, it's too late now, you're trapped." She locked the doors.

"I'm gonna go to sleep," Ryan laughed. "Wake me up when I'm dead."

"You can't go to sleep!" Lindsey told him. "I need someone to talk to."

"How far are we going?" Ryan asked.

"Like thirty minutes," she explained.

"That's a pretty far drive. What's the surprise?" Ryan asked.

"I'm not gonna tell you!" Lindsey said, almost offended.

Ryan laughed. "Can I get a hint?"

"No." she replied.

"You're the worst," he told her with a smile.

"You keep that up and I really might have to kill you," Lindsey laughed.

"All I want is a hint!" Ryan defended.

"All you have to do is be patient," she informed him.

"Be what?" he asked.

"Oh my god!" she sighed and laughed. "Just take a nap."

"Anything you want," Ryan said with a smile.

They talked for the rest of the car ride until they were outside the city.

"Just wait here until I get you," Lindsey said as she got out of the car.

"This really is kind of creepy," Ryan said to himself.

After about fifteen minutes Lindsey opened Ryan's door and helped him out of the car. They walked a short way and stopped.

"Ok, you can look," she said.

Ryan took off the blindfold and looked around. He was at the top of a small mountain outside the city. The stars lit up the sky like a fireworks festival. Standing up in front of him was a brand-new telescope aimed at the sky.

"What's this?" Ryan asked.

"For someone who loves the stars you don't have a telescope, so I got you one," Lindsey said happily.

"No way," Ryan said with happiness and a bit of awe in his voice. "How much did this thing cost?" he asked.

"I didn't know how to get the lens to work so you're gonna have to fix it. You remember how to use it from the one you had as a kid right?" she asked, completely ignoring the question.

"Come here," Ryan said softly. He leaned over and hugged her tightly. "Thank you so much. This is the coolest gift anybody has ever gotten me."

"I'm glad you like it," she smiled as she held him back. "Wanna show me some new stars?"

"Let's do it," Ryan said with a smile.

After getting the focus and small details set up the two watched the stars. They carried on for hours until they eventually sat back against some rocks and talked.

"This is so cool," Ryan said with awe. "I can see stars and planets I've never seen except for on shows or in books."

"It really is. I never actually looked at the stars until I met you. They're breathtaking," she said as she leaned against him.

"I could do this every night," Ryan said as he hugged her and gave her a kiss. "Thank you so much."

"You know I looked online and you could get a job at the observatory. They only require a two-year degree. You could do this all the time," Lindsey told him.

"I don't have time for school though. Or the money," he added.

"Well I looked up some financial aid and you might be able to get some. They also have night classes you can take," she explained.

"You really looked up all that stuff?" Ryan asked.

"Yea," Lindsey replied. "You love this, why not make it your life? It might be hard, but I will help you study and anything else that comes up. We can go talk to the school just to see what they say next time it rains."

Ryan sat in silence for a minute. He sighed. "You really think it could work?"

"We can try," she said happily. "Even if it takes longer or we have to find different ways to make it happen, why not try it? It's your life. You should do what you love."

"Maybe you're right," Ryan said. "I don't know, it always seemed like it was so far off, but two years seems to get shorter and shorter the older I get." He paused. "They have night classes I can take?"

"Yea I think so," she said excitely. "I can find out more info on everything if you want?"

"That's ok," Ryan said with a smile. "We can go next time it rains or were off. You don't have to do everything for me." He stared at her for a minute. "You really are the best thing that has ever happened to me."

"Aww! Stop it," Lindsey said as she buried her head in his shoulder.

Ryan put his arm around her. "Come on beautiful, it's getting cold. What time is it anyway?" he asked.

"I don't know, hold on," Lindsey replied as she grabbed her phone. "It's three," she told him.

"Oh hell," Ryan laughed.

"What's wrong?" Lindsey asked with a smile.

"Dads locked the doors by now and church is in the morning. If I wake him up he's gonna be pissed." Ryan explained.

"You didn't bring your keys?" she asked.

"I didn't bring anything!" Ryan laughed. "I didn't know I was going to the mountains for fifteen hours."

"It's ok don't worry you can stay at my place," Lindsey offered.

"Ok," he accepted. "I'm probably not getting up for church in time, so maybe we can go get breakfast or something when you wake up."

"When *I* wake up? What does that mean?" Lindsey asked.

Ryan laughed. "You always wake up after I do lazy bones," he joked as he poked her ribs.

"We'll see who's lazy when you have to walk back," she challenged.

"Well hell, I guess it would still be you, since I would be getting exercise," he laughed.

Lindsey just stared at him with angry eyes for a moment before hopping up and walking to the car.

"Oh come on!" Ryan laughed. "You said it not me!"

"Sorry I can't hear you!" Lindsey called back with a smile as she got in the car.

Chapter 20

Kelsey was cleaning up around The Coffee Hole talking to Tom while the store had settled down.

"I think you might be right," Kelsey laughed.

"Oh, I am," Tom said with a smile. "So, how is school going?"

"It's great actually," she replied. "I've just been learning so much and it's all becoming so much easier than it was before."

"That's great," Tom said happily. "I do bad news though," he added sadly.

"What?" she asked.

"You can't quit when you get this degree," Tom laughed. "I need you."

Kelsey laughed. "I still have another year until I finish, and that's if I pass all my classes. Then I need to pass boards, and thennn, I need to actually find a job. I'm not going anywhere any time soon."

"You'd be surprised how fast things go," Tom warned her.

"I'm ready for it to be over," Kelsey said as she sat down a sighed.

"Don't be," Tom said with a laugh. "The faster you get to the next stop the faster you leave the one you're at." He paused. "I know that sounds funny but think back to high school. Everybody wanted to leave so fast but now they miss it."

"I don't think we went to the same high school," Kelsey said dryly then laughed.

"Oh, you get the idea," Tom laughed. "You're gonna make memories in college, meet new people, have fun times. Even this place, I know hate it some days, but you will miss it too one day. So just enjoy all you have when you have it."

"I know," Kelsey smiled. "Thanks Tom."

Gerome sat at his desk looking over numbers for a big account again.

"Ay, where we eating lunch today boss?" Carver asked with a smile.

"I'm not your boss," Gerome laughed. "I told you to stop that. You're not making my reputation any better around here."

"I'm just saying, you work harder than our boss so why can't I call you boss?" Carver asked.

"You're gonna get me in trouble with all this," Gerome warned him.

"If I'm lying fire me," Carver smiled.

Just then Stacey came up to them.

"Hey, Mr. Whits wants to see you," she told Gerome.

"What did I tell you," Gerome said sarcastically to Carver. "Ok, thank you," he replied to Stacey.

After making his way to Mr. Whits' office Gerome had a seat.

"Thank you for your time Gerome. I realize it is close to lunch. I wanted to catch you before," Whits informed him.

"It's no problem at all sir," Gerome replied. "How can I help you?" he asked.

"Well as you know we have been looking to advance one of our best employees to a management position due to the expansion," Mr. Whits said seriously. "I would like to extend the offer to you first. This would be a big responsibility, you would be ultimately in charge of your entire department's accounts and employees. Now of course you wouldn't have to do the daily work. You would be mainly in charge of important accounts, and making sure productivity stays high. You have actually been in charge of some of these responsibilities for some time now am I correct?"

"Yes sir, I have been doing what I can to learn more and be capable of handling more managerial tasks should the need arise," Gerome explained.

"Excellent! That's why you were my number one candidate for the position," Whits said with a smile. "What do you think? Does this sound like a direction you would like to take?"

"Yes sir, more than anything," Gerome replied seriously.

"I'll send the emails to confirm it this afternoon," Mr. Whits said. "You will of course receive a two dollar raise. We don't have a new office for you just yet, but don't worry, that will come soon."

"That's no problem, thank you for the opportunity sir," Gerome replied.

"No, thank you," Whits replied with a big smile.

Alex sat at his stall happily looking into the crowd. People walked by eyeing his paintings as they passed. He waved and some waved back while others would stop to admire his work.

"I love to see this," an elderly woman said to Alex as she walked past. "People are so caught up with technology, for a young man like you to be here is nice. Kids today are so worried about their phones and video games that they might forget how to paint one day.

"Thank you," Alex replied cheerfully. And yea, it does suck, but that's why my job and other artists is to keep the spirit alive!"

The woman smiled. "Well thank you for your good work."

"I do what I can," Alex smiled. "Would you like a painting?"

"I don't think I'll get one today, but I need to tell my daughter to come look at your work. She loves art and would probably take half the stall home with her," the woman laughed.

"Please tell her," Alex laughed. "I would love to sell half my collection."

"Well take care," the woman smiled as she turned to leave.

"You too," Alex smiled.

Alex returned home that night and on the kitchen table was a letter.

"Is this it?" he asked with excitement. "It is!"

Dear Mr. Rings,

We love your art, and you are a very talented artist. We regret to inform you that we have decided to move in a different direction regarding the position. We appreciate your time and wish you the best of luck in your career.

Mr. Walter

Alex slowly let the letter and his hand fall to his side as he stared blankly at the table. After nearly a minute he shook his head slowly and threw the letter in the trash. He walked to his room and closed the door before falling on his bed and forcing himself to sleep.

Chapter 21

Alex walked into The Coffee Hole at 2 am. The place was quiet except for the music softly playing from the speakers.

"Alex! Hey," Kelsey said as he walked in. "I feel like I haven't seen you in forever."

"Hey, sorry," Alex replied with a smile.

"How have you been?" she asked. "Did you start that new job yet?"

"No," Alex said with a disappointed frown.

"Oh… I'm sorry," Kelsey responded quietly.

The smell of alcohol was in the air by the time Alex made it to the register.

"It's no problem," he assured her with a forced smile.

"What can I get you?" Kelsey asked.

Alex looked over the menu. "Just let me get a large coffee with extra espresso."

"Ok," Kelsey said with a concerned look. "Not the usual?" she smiled.

"Nah, not tonight," Alex replied with a smile.

She made him the drink and he went to sit down.

After a minute or two Kelsey went and sat with him.

"You can talk to me if you want," she told him. "You're always there for me to talk to, and I know you don't drink espresso," she added softly.

Alex froze for half a second and quickly recovered.

"It's nothing," he said with a smile. "I'm just tired mostly, I stayed up trying some new paint out."

Kelsey looked at him.

Alex sighed and looked at the ground. "I got rejected again. For the thousandth time. I'm just not good enough."

"You are good enough though," she reassured him. "You've sold tons of paintings."

"Mostly to friends and people who don't even know art. I spend thirty or forty hours on a painting and it's a waste nobody wants. Then I spend an hour on one and that is mediocre at best and everyone loves it," he replied.

"But they still love it. Isn't that good?" she asked.

"That's like your parents praising you for your nice furniture set up in your living room while they casually ignore the entire house you built," Alex explained.

"Some people just don't see it," Kelsey said. "I don't know a thing about art, but I know some of your paintings are really beautiful. I don't care how long they took."

"It's more than that though," he said. "This life sucks." He paused for a moment and shook his head. "I moved here when I was a kid, me and my mom. She loved to paint. We would always paint together, and she would teach me cool new things every day. Her paintings made me so happy and I asked her why she wasn't an artist like the guys I saw in books, why did she have to work at that stupid warehouse all the time. She would smile and say, 'I have to make sure I take care of you silly'. I would argue saying how if she just sold paintings she could do it, and we could paint all day, not just the days she had off. She would always just smile and dismiss it. One day on the way to work she was hit by some asshole that was late to his job. They took her to the hospital, but she was dead by the time they arrived." Tears started to well up in his eyes. "All I could think was if she just stayed home, if she just painted more, if she didn't go to that stupid job!" Tears started to fall, and he quickly wiped them up. "They moved me to my grandma's house, she was the only family I really had left. From then on, I promised myself I would never let that happen again. I would show her what we could do, and that life wouldn't have to be this way. I practiced all the time and made sure I was good enough to make it. It wasn't until a couple years ago when my grandma passed away that I realized how wrong I was. With no fallback left I happily looked forward thinking 'this was my time'. I was broke, homeless, and almost died on the streets within six months. I finally found some shitty part time job that would take me. Then I rented the dirtiest studio apartment money could buy. I gave up painting. Mom was right. You can't make it as an artist with nothing. But I couldn't stop, I tried again, and failed again. I ruined my life. I failed my way through high school, thinking I was going to paint my way to success. I had no education, a dead-end job, no skills, and no success painting. I thought about ending it all so many times. That feeling of being alone in a cold dark apartment, with nothing to comfort you but the empty bottles that sat on the floor as your head starts to spin. I just couldn't do it though. I came so close, but something inside wouldn't let me. So I just drank myself to sleep most nights. One day I met a guy who sold paintings at the flea market. We talked, and I told him about my paintings. He said I could sell mine there. He moved and left me his stall, paid through the year, and I got lucky finding a roommate. I thought that was my time, that I had finally made it." Alex stopped and shook his head, still looking at the ground. "It's all over again. I can't afford the stall, I can't afford rent, I can't afford anything. I'm just glad I didn't have a kid and ruin their life too."

The two sat in silence for a moment.

"I'm sorry," Kelsey said. "I never knew. You always seemed to have your life so... together. You're always so happy."

"I have to be," Alex replied. "The world needs a light. They need to be happy and be reminded that there is more to life than just money. That your dreams shouldn't have to die... I guess I was just lying to them."

"You're not though!" Kelsey argued as a flood of emotion came over her face. "I really do love your paintings. You do make the world a better place, people love you, people need you. How many people do you see smile when you show up. You have a lot of friends that would help you," she explained.

"They have their own problems," Alex said seriously. "They have bills, kids, houses to buy. If somebody can't afford to buy a painting and actually get something in return, they are not going to just pay me for nothing." He paused. "And you know the worst part." The tears came back. "I'm just going to do this all over again. This stupid ass dream is never going to die and I'm just going to let it destroy me, over and over. I just smile and waste my time repeating this cycle over and over." He stood up. "I'm sorry," he said before he walked out into the night.

Chapter 22

Kelsey was hastily getting ready for work when Ashley came up to her.

"Don't you have class today?" she asked.

"Yea, but somebody else quit and I've been having to work non-stop," Kelsey replied with a very tired and irritated tone.

"This semester is almost over, you don't have a test or anything do you?" Ashley asked.

"No. Just one project but I can turn it in this weekend online," Kelsey explained.

"Ok," Ashley said skeptically. "Just try and remember this job isn't that important. You can't just work every day because other people quit. It's not your responsibility. You can only do so much before you ruin your own life helping someone else."

"I know, I know," Kelsey replied. "They just really need help and it's only for a little bit."

"Ok, try not to kill yourself. Love you," Ashley said as Kelsey moved to the door.

"Love you too," Kelsey replied as she left.

Saturday came, and Kelsey was leaving work that night.

"Bye!" she called to everybody.

"Bye! Go enjoy your time off! And don't forget to turn in that project," Amber reminded her.

"Trust me," Kelsey said seriously, "I won't." She smiled and left for home.

Kelsey got home and hopped in her bed. After turning on her laptop she went to her schools teaching website.

'We are experiencing problems. Please try again later'

The screen was white with this error message.

"No, no, no," Kelsey said as she refreshed it. "Come on."

'We are experiencing problems. Please try again later'

'We are experiencing problems. Please try again later'

'We are experiencing problems. Please try again later'

'We are experiencing problems. Please try again later'

'We are experiencing problems. Please try again later'

"Please, not tonight!" she pleaded.

'We are experiencing problems. Please try again later'

'We are experiencing problems. Please try again later'

She looked at the time. 11:20

"I've got forty minutes. Please fix by then."

The time passed, and it was 11:58.

"Please!" Kelsey said, getting more frantic.

'We are experiencing problems. Please try again later'

'We are experiencing problems. Please try again later'

'We are experiencing problems. Please try again later'

'We are experiencing problems. Please try again later'

The time hit 12:00

"Noo!" she yelled and slammed the laptop shut. Sadness swept over her face.

"I'm gonna fail."

"Hey is everything ok?" Ashley asked as she opened the door.

"No, it's not," Kelsey said.

"What's wrong?" Ashley asked as she moved over to the bed.

"The stupid site is down, and I couldn't turn in my project and now I'm going to fail! That was forty percent of my grade!" she said franticly.

"It's ok, just email your teacher. I'm sure you can explain what happened. This wasn't your fault," Ashley assured her.

Kelsey started to calm down a bit. She opened the laptop and went to her email. She had a couple of unopened emails. One was from her professor.

Dear students,

   Some of you missed class today. Your final project needs to be turned in by Thursday. The MySchoolLearning site will be down this weekend and I cannot accept projects through email. I apologize for this inconvenience, but my hands are tied. Thank you again for your understanding and I hope all of you enjoy your break!

Dr. King

Tears started to fill Kelsey's eyes as she read the email.

"Hey what happened?" Ashley asked softly. She leaned in and put her hand on Kelsey's back.

"I failed," Kelsey said and broke down. Tears came falling down as she leaned forward and put her head in her hands.

"What happened? You can't turn it in late?" Ashley asked rubbing her back.

"No," Kelsey replied. "I can't turn it in at all!"

"It's ok," Ashley assured her. "It's just one class, you can bounce back easy."

"I'm gonna lose my scholarship now, and not be able to pay for school, and have to take extra classes to graduate on time! It's not ok!" Tears poured out as she wept, curled up on her bed. "All because of this stupid job! All people have do is show up for work. It's not that hard! But no, now life is ruined because of some dead-end job and some dead-end losers that work there!"

"It's ok," Ashley continued. "You can still appeal to keep your scholarship. I had to do it before."

"It's not like I have perfect grades," Kelsey argued. "They are just gonna see that, and the dropped class, and now this and say no."

"I promise it's gonna be ok," Ashley said softly. "Come here." She grabbed Kelsey and held her close.

Kelsey leaned over and continued to cry.

"You just have to calm down. We won't know anything until Monday, right?" Ashley asked

"I guess," Kelsey replied, sniffing back some tears.

"Just relax and try to get some sleep. You worked all day, didn't you? You just need some rest, ok?" Ashley said.

"I guess," Kelsey said as she wiped her face and began to calm down.

"It's gonna be ok, I promise. You just had a long day," Ashley assured her.

"Thank you," Kelsey replied softly.

"It's ok, I've been here before. I know how stressful it can be. Just think, if my dumbass can make it so can you," Ashley laughed.

"You're not dumb," Kelsey sniffed.

"Aww. Even when life has you down you're still the most supportive friend I could ever ask for," Ashley said as she squeezed Kelsey.

Kelsey let out a small laugh.

"I heard that!" Ashley said with a smile and started to poke Kelsey in the ribs.

Kelsey jumped up and started squirming to get away while she started laughing.

"That's better," Ashley smiled as she let up the attack.

Kelsey wiped her eyes and fully calmed down.

"Thank you," she said. "You really are the best friend I could ever ask for."

"You've done the same for me," Ashley replied. "Now get some sleep ok," she said as she patted the bed.

Kelsey got comfortable and Ashley walked to the door.

"Night!" Ashley said.

"Night," Kelsey replied softly.

Ashley turned out the lights and Kelsey fell asleep almost immediately.

Monday came, and Kelsey had to work the morning shift. She quickly moved back and forth making coffee and taking orders.

"Ugh, where are all of these people coming from?" she asked herself.

The shop was full of people and a long line was waiting to be served.

"Excuse me miss! This was supposed to be no cream!" an angry customer called to Kelsey from the other side of the counter.

"I'm sorry," Kelsey replied. "I can make you a fresh cup."

"Do we have any more large lids?" Amber asked

"I'm sure we do!" Kelsey replied. "You know where to look."

Amber gave her an irritated look and went to find lids.

"I've been waiting for five minutes! Where is my coffee? I'm going to be late!" the man demanded.

"I'm sorry! It's right here!" Kelsey explained as she quickly tried to put the lid on. She tried to hand the man the coffee while he quickly reached for it. The two bumped hands and the coffee spilt on the man's suit.

"Ahh! You have got to be kidding me!" he shouted.

"I'm so sorry!" Kelsey pleaded.

"Sorry? I have a fucking meeting in twenty minutes!" the man said angrily.

Kelsey tried to apologize, but the man continued.

"What the fuck is wrong with you? All you have to do is make coffee! Some of us have real jobs!"

Kelsey looked around at all the people in line staring at her. Tears started to form in her eyes. She threw down the apron and the man continued.

"Where the fuck do you think you're going? Somebody is going to pay for this!" he yelled.

Kelsey ran to the door pushing aside people as tears streamed down her face. She ran to her car and left.

After speeding home Kelsey got home and ran to her room. She slammed the door behind her and made her way to her bed taking only a second to throw off her shoes.

"Why!" she yelled as she sobbed into her pillow.

She cried until her eyes slowly closed and she drifted off to sleep.

Chapter 23

"No way! That's awesome!" Demetry said.

"Yea! I finally made another big step in life!" Gerome happily replied.

"Your own office?" Digs mused. "Sure you can handle that?"

"Yea right," Gerome said. "I've been doing my bosses work for a while now, it's about time I get his position."

"I'm proud of you man," Demetry said seriously.

"Thanks D. I'm gonna go tell my mom the good news tomorrow," Gerome said.

"She's gonna be so pumped," Demetry said excitedly.

"I hope so," Gerome replied with a smile.

Gerome pulled up to an old looking house on the far side of the city. Neighbors and people passing by eyed him with suspicious looks. He got out and walked up to the house. The screen door had a hole in it. Gerome pulled it open and knocked on the wooden door. After a minute a woman answered the door.

"Hey baby! I was wondering when you would get here," the woman said as she moved in for a hug.

"Yea, sorry, I got stuck in traffic," Gerome explained with a smile as he hugged her.

"Come in, come in. Have you ate yet?" she asked as they walked inside.

"I could always eat if you're cooking," Gerome laughed. "I thought you said you were gonna get that door fixed?" he asked seriously. "I told you months ago I would buy you a new one."

"That's ok, you save your money," she replied with a smile. "Besides your father said he would fix it."

"Mary who is that?" a voice called from the living room.

"It's Gerome! I told you he was coming by," she called back.

"Nice to see the busy businessman has time for his family twice a year!" the man called back. "You bring me a new car?" he laughed.

"Good to see you too Dad," Gerome said dryly as he walked to the kitchen with is mother. He sat down while she moved to start cooking. "I've got big news," Gerome said happily.

"Oh! More good news?" Mary asked with a smile. "You found you a woman to settle down with?"

Gerome laughed. "No, but I got a big promotion at work. I'm gonna be head of my department," he explained.

"You better stop," Mary said with a smile. "You're gonna be a manager at this big corporation?" she asked happily.

"Yep," Gerome said proudly. "Getting my own office and everything."

"Come give me a hug!" Mary said as she opened her arms. Gerome stood and embraced her. "I'm so proud of you! You worked so hard and you're getting so far in life." She stepped back. "Roger! Come hear what your son did!" she called to his father.

"Tell him to bring his ass here, the game is on," Roger replied from the living room.

His mother sighed. "Just go tell him, I'll start lunch," she smiled.

Gerome walked in to the living room. His father sat on the couch with a half empty forty ounce in his hand.

"What's so special?" Roger asked. "You buy a nice big house and gonna move in with a nice uptown girl?"

"I got a promotion at work, I'm the boss now," Gerome informed him.

"Wow, good job. Now how does that affect me?" his father asked. "You plan on giving me some money?"

"I told you guys before, I would help you if you ever needed anything," Gerome said irritation swept into his voice. "You seem to be doing fine though," he added with noticeable attitude.

"The fuck's that supposed to mean?" Roger asked.

"Nothing. Just get to sit around, no job, mom does all the work, drink all day, relax. Must be nice. Some of us have to work for a living," Gerome explained.

"Hold up. Number one, this is my house, and I don't know who the fuck you're talking to like that," Roger said as he leaned up. "And number two, what we do is none of your business. You don't pay our bills."

"I don't know why I even bother coming back here," Gerome said slightly raising his voice. "You're just a piece of shit."

Roger stood up. "Who the fuck you calling a piece of shit white boy? Maybe you forgot who raised your ass and fed you when you were in diapers."

"Stop it," Mary called as she walked into the room.

"White boy? So I'm a fucking white boy because I'm successful and dress nice? Maybe I should have joined a gang and ended up shot or in jail! Would that make me black enough for you? Would that make you proud?" Gerome yelled as the two men got closer to each other.

"You're what's wrong with the black community! You're the reason kids never grow up to be what they could be. You're the reason why people thing being black means being a thug! Why the one kid who actually tries to make something of himself gets made fun of and beat up!"

The two men were eye to eye now. Mary tried to pull them apart.

"Say one more thing and I'll bust your ass right here," Roger challenged.

"Stop it!" Mary yelled as she tried to push Roger away from Gerome.

"Bitch!" Roger yelled as he pushed her back into the wall, knocking a picture off the wall.

Gerome's eyes filled with rage as he rushed his father. He swung and hit him in the cheek. Roger stumbled, and Gerome followed with another swing. Roger fell to the ground and Gerome followed. He hit him again and again.

"DON'T YOU EVER!" he punched the man. "EVER!" he punched once more. "TOUCH HER AGAIN!"

"Stop it!" Mary yelled. "Stop it!" she desperately tried to pull Gerome back.

"I'll fucking kill you!" Gerome yelled as he hit the man's now bloody face one last time. He finally stopped and stood up. Mary rushed to Roger's side with tears in her eyes.

"I'm done," Gerome said to his mom. "For as long as you keep this piece of shit around I'm never coming back here again!" He stormed out of the house, got inside his car, and left.

Chapter 24

Ryan sat talking to Luis on their lunch break.

"You think I could go to school? Maybe do something else?" Ryan asked casually.

"Shit, I don't see why not," Luis replied. "I guess anything is possible. What do you want to do?" he asked.

"I thought about trying to become an astrologist," Ryan explained.

"Shit!" Luis laughed. "That's some serious shit. You sure you smart enough for that?"

Ryan laughed. "Hell, I don't even know. I do like it though."

"Well then go for it. This fucking job sucks anyway," Luis encouraged him.

"I'll probably mention it to my dad tonight. I don't think he would care as long as I took night classes and made it to work," Ryan explained.

"Yea, I don't see why he would, as long as you got your work done," Luis agreed.

Ryan sat down to eat with his parents that evening. His mom was talking about her day at work. When she finished Ryan cut in.

"Hey Dad," he said. "What do you think about me going back to school?"

"School?" Stan asked. "For what?"

"I was thinking for astrology," Ryan explained.

"Astrology?" his mom asked with a laugh.

"This is because of that girl you've been dating, isn't it?" his dad asked.

"No, it's something I've thought about before," Ryan defended.

"Do they even have jobs open doing whatever it is they do?" Rebecca asked.

"They do," Ryan told them. "After I finish school I might be able to get a job at the observatory."

"Might?" his father asked. He sighed and continued. "Look, I think you need to not spend so much time with that girl. You haven't been the same the past couple of months."

"Her name is Lindsey," Ryan said getting defensive. "And what's that supposed to mean?"

"Before you go getting pissed off, nothing I'm gonna say isn't true," Stan said seriously. "You have been staying out late, your missing church, you show up to work tired, and now you want to quit for some random thing."

"I'm..." Ryan started to say.

"I wasn't finished," Stan said, cutting him off. "I don't think you understand what it looks like on me. If you show up late it falls on me, if you don't pull your weight it falls on me, what you do affects me. I pretty much handed you a job because you're my son. Now yes, you've earned it by all the work you put in over the years, but is that something you really want to just throw away? We have given you a couple extra years to stay with us, but one of these days you're going to need to support yourself. I don't think some girl who is trying to get you to throw away a stable life for some random job has your best interests in mind."

"She's not..." Ryan tried to defend again before his mom jumped in.

"We're not saying she's a bad girl," Rebecca reassured him. "She seems like a sweet girl. We just want you to think about your future. Just be careful is all we're saying."

"Ok," Ryan said quietly.

"Don't be mad honey," his mom continued. "We want you two to be happy together I promise."

"I just think she's still young and doesn't really know what it takes too raise a family and get a house," Stan explained. "You know better than that though. We raised you with a good head on your shoulders. You two will turn out fine, just stay focused. If you want to marry this girl and have a life you can't do that by making risky decisions."

"Yes sir, sorry," Ryan said.

"Don't be sorry, just be mindful," Stan replied.

"Thanks dad," Ryan said.

Ryan got off work and walked to his truck. The sky was grey and looked like rain could come at any time. Lindsey was waiting for him when he got there.

"Hey cutie," she said with a smile. "How was work?"

"Tiring," Ryan laughed.

"Wanna get some food? You probably haven't eaten since lunch, have you?" she asked.

"You read my mind," Ryan said with a smile, then leaned in and kissed her.

"Hop in," Lindsey said as she turned and walked to the driver side of her car. "I'll drive."

The two got in and she drove down the road.

"Burgers ok?" she asked.

"You know that you get to pick, and I have to be happy with that," Ryan laughed.

"Hey, I still need to at least ask," Lindsey smiled. "Oh! I think they said it's gonna rain tomorrow. We can go to the school in the morning. I'll be off," she added with excitement.

Ryan froze for a second. "That's ok," he said softly.

"What's ok?" she asked.

"The school," Ryan explained. "We don't have to go."

"We don't know when it will be a good day to go after this," Lindsey argued. "Why not tomorrow?"

"I just don't feel like it," Ryan replied.

"Oh, come on lazy," Lindsey laughed. "It's only for one day. How can you be my handsome star man if you can't get out of bed for one day of work?"

"It's fine," Ryan replied with a serious tone.

"What's wrong?" Lindsey asked, getting concerned.

"Nothing," Ryan said. "I'm just not gonna go."

"Like at all? Ever?" she asked.

"No, probably not," Ryan explained.

"But why?" Lindsey asked. "I thought this was something you really wanted?"

"Well I changed my mind, I already have a job," Ryan said.

"What's wrong?" she pleaded. "You can talk to me."

"Nothing's wrong!" Ryan snapped at her. "Just stop with the stupid star shit."

"What are you talking about?" Lindsey asked getting more and more stressed. "I thought you were excited about this? What changed?"

"You were the one excited about it. You're the one who said all that stuff, not me. I have a good job and you just want me to throw it all away for some fucking pipe dream!" Ryan said getting aggressive.

Tears started to well up in Lindsey's eyes as she tried to fight them back.

"I just wanted you to be happy. Why are you yelling at me?" she asked as her voice cracked.

"I was happy the way I was," Ryan said.

Lindsey broke down and started crying.

"So I've just ruined your life? Everything was better before you met me?" she asked. "You made me so happy. Every time your eyes would light up when you got excited about the stars. You showed me so many cool new things. I really thought I was making your life better!" she wiped tears from her face. Ryan continued to look away. She stopped the car. "You think I have dreams like that? I don't have anything! I work a regular job and live a regular life! You gave me something to be excited about. All I wanted to do was make sure I could see that spark in your eyes over and over as we made your dreams come true. Now it's just over? You're just gonna throw it all away to stay at a back-breaking job you hate?"

"I think we need to take a break," Ryan said as his voice cracked.

"So that's it?" Lindsey asked as the tears started to rush even faster. "It's all over?"

Ryan started to shake as he looked out the window. "How am I supposed to know!" he turned as tears started running down his cheeks. "You think this is fucking easy for me?" he opened the door as rain drops began to fall from the sky. He slammed the door shut and started walking to his truck.

Chapter 24

Kelsey laid on her bed staring at the ceiling. She picked up her phone and looked at it. After a second or two she put it back down and sighed. Minutes passed, and she picked up the phone again, this time scrolling to 'Mom' in the contacts. She pressed the call button and held the phone to her ear.

"Hey sweetie!" her mom answered the phone.

"Hey Mom," Kelsey replied sadly.

"What's up?" Diane asked with concern.

"Is Dad around?" Kelsey asked.

"No, he's at work right now. Is everything ok?" her mom asked.

Kelsey sighed and paused for a second. "I might need to move back home."

"Move back? What happened honey? Is everything ok?" Diane asked quickly.

"I quit my job, and I'm pretty sure I lost all my financial aid for school," Kelsey said quietly.

"You quit? What happened?" she asked.

"I was working too much, and I didn't check my email, and missed the most important project in my class, and then spilt coffee all over a customer, and I just couldn't take it!" Kelsey spoke faster and faster as she explained what happened. "I'm sorry! I tried my best."

"Easy honey," her mom comforted her. "That sounds like a lot at once. Let's slow down. One at a time. Did they send you a letter or email saying you lost your financial aid?"

"No," Kelsey said quietly.

"Then you haven't lost it yet," Diane assured her.

"But they said I need to have a certain GPA, and not fail, and..." Kelsey started to argue.

"They say a lot of things," her mother replied with a smile. "Even if it's gone we can make plans for that. Now what happened at work?"

"I just dumped coffee on a guy and walked out," Kelsey said dryly.

Her mother chuckled. "I don't think you just threw a cup at someone and stormed out. It was an accident, wasn't it?"

Kelsey paused. "I mean yea, but I still just walked out and ruined his suit," she added as she started to relax.

"Have you talked to your boss? Tony, right?" her mother asked.

"No," Kelsey said quietly.

"You think he might be waiting for you to come up there and talk to him?" Diane asked.

"It's already been a week," Kelsey said.

"That's ok, I've seen people go a lot longer than that. Trust me," her mother assured her. "And even if you lose the job, we can find others. Me and your father can help you until you get on your feet."

"I don't want to tell Dad," Kelsey explained.

"How can he help you if he doesn't know what's wrong?" her mother asked.

"I'm not supposed to need help. He's always so proud of me, and tells me how great I'm doing. I want to do it on my own like he did. He didn't need help like this," Kelsey told her.

Her mother started laughing. "Sweetie are you kidding me? Your father failed out of community college and had to wash cars to get back on his feet, in his first year," she added. "You're already doing much better than he did. That's one reason he's so proud. Nobody ever gets it right on the first try. That's why you have us."

141

"I guess," Kelsey said quietly.

"Don't you 'I guess' me!" Diane replied. "Do you need anything right now? You have enough money for food?"

"Yea," Kelsey said.

"Ok. I want you to send an email, or go to the school and let me know what the situation is, and then we can make a plan if you need some help ok? Then I want you to go talk to your boss. Does he work today?" her mother asked.

"No, but I don't know, because I was supposed to work today," Kelsey explained.

"Well find out when he's gonna be there and make sure you go talk to him," Diane said.

"Ok," Kelsey said.

They sat in silence for a moment.

"You want me to let you go?" her mother asked.

"Yea, I guess," Kelsey replied.

"I love you," Diane said. "Don't beat yourself up."

"Love you too, I won't" Kelsey replied a bit more happily than she had been. "Thank you for all your help."

"Anytime, Bye sweetie."

"Bye Mom."

Chapter 25

Gerome sat at his desk blankly looking at his computer screen. He hadn't actually done any work in almost thirty minutes.

"Hey man, you ok?" Carver asked him.

"Yea," Gerome replied. "Just didn't get enough sleep."

"You're the boss now," Carver laughed, "just take a nap."

"Yea right," Gerome smiled. "I don't own the place yet. I'm just ready for this day to be over with." He frowned.

"I know that feeling," Carver said seriously. "I feel it every day that I step in this building," he laughed.

"You're a mess," Gerome laughed.

The two got back to work and they finished the day. After work Gerome went downtown to the pizza shop Demetry worked at. Demetry was sitting outside as Gerome came up to the building and joined him.

"What's up G," Demetry said with a smile.

"Sup man," Gerome replied unenthusiastically.

"You good?" Demetry asked him.

"I don't even know anymore," Gerome answered. "I think I hate my job."

"I thought you just got promoted?" Demetry asked.

"It's not like it really mattered," Gerome explained. "I got it, but now I'm doing so much work and they didn't even give me my office yet, and that raise was worthless. I already had more than enough money."

"Dang man," Demetry replied.

"And the people are all shitty," Gerome continued. "They are passive aggressive shit talkers who secretly hate everyone else. They invite you to parties and get togethers to drink and have fun. Then next week they all spread rumors and talk bad about the person who got too drunk. Some are stuck up assholes. I just don't feel like I even belong there."

"Sounds stressful," Demetry sympathized with him.

"It's not even stressful," Gerome replied. "I'm not stressed, I'm just tired of that place. I just don't want to be there anymore."

"Where do you want to go?" Demetry asked.

"I don't even know," Gerome said as he leaned back. "I just miss the days when life was fun. When we all just hung out and played music and really enjoyed life."

"You can always come do dishes," Demetry laughed. "We have lots of fun."

"Gerome laughed. "If only."

"Why can't you?" Demetry asked seriously.

"I can't just quit my job and waste all that school, and money, and promotion. Besides, I can't afford to live on that job anyway." He paused. "But it would be nice."

"We all share a place right now and it helps keep the bills pretty cheap. We could look for a place with another room for you," Demetry explained.

"Is it really ok to be a bum dishwasher as a career?" Gerome asked.

"You're only a bum if you don't work for what you have," Demetry said. "Same thing with being a skateboarder," he pointed at a kid skating down the sidewalk. "You're only a punk kid if you choose to be. Picking up a board doesn't make you one. I've never understood why people always make things synonymous when they have nothing to do with each other. Like how all metal bands are Satanists, or all southern people are racist..."

"Or all black people are thugs," Gerome added as he stared off into the city.

"Exactly," Demetry said. "It's up to us to live our own lives the way we want them. If we let other people decide for us, then we are just going to be miserable."

Gerome sighed and looked up at the sky. "When we were in high school we were branded as punks. People hated us and thought we were always up to no good. Granted we were sometimes," he smiled. "But most of the time we just wanted to have fun. It wasn't until the start of eleventh grade that I really felt like I needed to change. People just saw me as another black kid getting in trouble. They literally turned me into a statistic when they would talk about me. I didn't want that for my life. I didn't want to be a loser in a band. I wanted to make my parents proud, I wanted to show the world what a black man could really be. I just wanted to prove them wrong so badly." He paused. "And now look at me. I made it. I'm the boss. And for what?"

"I'm sorry man," Demetry said as he put his hand around Gerome's shoulder. "I never knew it hit you that hard. You seemed so passionate about your future."

"I was," Gerome replied, "but it wasn't my future. It was the future everyone else wanted for me."

"We live on a very fine line," Demetry said seriously. "We are always one drink away from a bad decision, one party away from a drug addiction, one tempting girl away from an STD or a kid, one show away from having it all fall apart and becoming the things they told us we would be. Look at how many people this lifestyle swallows up. How many people in our shoes take it too far and lose everything. It's up to us to be mindful of that and remember who we are when things get crazy. It's not easy, but I guess that's why they say it's a far trip to the peak if you want to rock and roll."

Gerome chuckled. "Honestly, I don't even know anymore. I just want to go to sleep and wake up when my life is together."

"Live can be hard to figure out. I had my battle and made my choice," Demetry explained. "I still wonder if it was the right one, but I'm happy here. As long as we're happy what more really matters?"

Gerome sighed and looked up again. "Maybe you're right."

Chapter 26

Ryan laid in his bed looking at the starry painting that hung on his wall. He stared at it for minutes before he stood up.

"Ugh," he said as he walked to the wall and took the painting off. He put the painting in his truck and left.

Ryan was walking into The Coffee Hole when he seen Digs.

"Hey, what's up Ryan?" Digs greeted him.

"Hey Digs," Ryan replied. "You seen Alex?"

"Not since yesterday, why what's up?" he asked.

"I just need to give him back this painting," Ryan explained.

"Why's that? I thought you liked it?" Digs asked.

Ryan paused. "I just… it's over," he said. "I talked to my parents and I don't need stupid dreams like this to mess up my future."

Digs looked at him seriously then smiled and shook his head. "Hold on bud. I've got a little time left on break, and D would kill me if I didn't stop you."

"What are you talking about?" Ryan asked.

"Sit down," Digs said as he pulled out a chair and sat.

"It's fine," Ryan replied as he sat down. "I just don't want the painting anymore."

"First thing is Alex has been going through a rough time from what I heard. If you tell him his painting sucks, it's really gonna hurt. Second thing is you still love that painting, but you were told by your parents it's bad, weren't you?" Digs asked.

"No, they never said anything about it," Ryan replied.

"A painting isn't a stupid dream that ruins your future, and you would never say that about your own dreams," Digs explained. "What happened?"

Ryan paused. "Nothing really. I just mentioned going to school and being an astrologist to them and they said no."

"Ok, so they think it's a bad idea," Digs said. "But what about the people who think it's a good one? Your girlfriend supports you, doesn't she?"

"She's actually not my girlfriend anymore," Ryan explained. "We got into it and were taking a break."

"What was the fight about?" Digs asked.

"Just all this stupid stuff," Ryan said.

Digs sighed. "Ok, look. Don't get mad at me and listen until I'm done ok. I don't want to have to fight you in this shop over some small shit. Your parents are wrong. They are ruining your life and holding you back. I'm not saying they are dumb or anything like that, but they are just too worried about protecting you. You know D's parents pretty much disowned him in high school. They said that the band he was in was for devil worshipers, they said he needed to go to college and make something of his life, they said he was a bad kid and constantly talked down to him for hanging out with his friends. They had a vision for his life and it wasn't what he wanted. They weren't wrong, those weren't bad things they wanted, but that's not how you raise a child. Parents try to live their children's lives for them, forgetting that we are all people with feelings and dreams of our own. The point I'm trying to make is don't let them have that much control over you. I know it's easier said than done. I still remember nights where Demetry would come over to my house in tears saying that his parents hated him. Before he moved in with me and my family he thought he was going to be miserable forever, even thought about killing himself. The feeling that you're stupid or worthless in your parent's eyes can really take its toll. Then there is the battle with having to kill all your own dreams and desires to make them happy. Like this painting that I know you love. You might not be able to tell your parents no, but if you don't this isn't going to get any better. Keep that painting and talk to your girlfriend. I don't want to see this happen to someone else."

Ryan just sat at the table in silence.

Digs stood up and walked to him, putting his hand on Ryan's shoulder. "I know that seemed harsh. I'm not good at advice. I'm just gonna tell you how it is. If you need help go talk to D, he's lived through the same problems. Take care man."

Digs left and Ryan sat at the table.

Chapter 27

Alex walked into The Coffee Hole and made his way to the counter.

"Alex," Tom called from the other side of the room. "Come here for a minute."

Alex walked over and had a seat. "What's up old man?" he laughed.

"Is everything ok?" Tom asked seriously.

"Yea," Alex said uneasily. "Why do you ask?"

"I just wanted to check. I haven't seen you around as often," Tom said.

"I've just been painting a lot," Alex explained.

"Oh, I didn't see you at your stall last Sunday either," Tom added.

"Yea, I was just busy that day. I really gotta go," Alex said. "Thanks for checking on me." He turned to leave.

"Hold on, I need your help. Kelsey quit," Tom informed him.

"She what?" Alex asked.

"She walked out, and I haven't heard from her. I need someone to work in her place," Tom told him. "I know you have a lot going on with your paintings, but you know most of the customers and are familiar with the place. Would you be willing to help?"

"Yea, I could help," Alex replied.

"What days could you work?" Tom asked.

"Any day, any time," Alex said with a bit of excitement.

"Even third?" Tom asked seriously.

"No problem! I don't have a life anyway," Alex laughed.

Tom smiled. "Alright, thank you Mr. Rings. Your first day is Wednesday at seven in the morning."

"Thanks man! I'll be here," Alex replied happily.

Kelsey opened the front door to The Coffee Hole slowly. She looked around as she slowly approached the counter. She made eye contact with Tom and half smiled.

Tom nodded, and she sat down until he walked out and joined her.

"Hey," she said quietly.

"Hey," Tom replied.

After a short silence Kelsey spoke.

"I'm sorry."

"It's ok," Tom said. "Is everything ok?"

"I just got so stressed with school, and I missed a project, and failed a class because I picked up that shift," Kelsey explained. "Then I accidently spilt coffee and I just..."

"Kelsey, why would you take extra shifts if you had to be at school? You told me that the semester was over and that you were free," Tom scolded her.

"You needed people because Jason quit and I..." she started to explain.

"I don't care if I had the whole crew quit and I have to close the shop for the day. You need to be at school, that is your future," Tom explained.

"I'm sorry," Kelsey said sadly.

"It's ok," Tom sighed. "Just be honest with me next time. If you don't tell people what's really going on you're going to hurt yourself. Remember to take care of yourself before you help others. I know that sounds terrible, but what matters most is that you get your degree and focus on your future, not some coffee shop you won't be at a couple years from now."

"Yea," Kelsey said as she looked away.

"Your parents told you the same thing, didn't they?" Tom laughed.

"Yea," Kelsey smiled.

"Do you want to come back to work?" Tom asked.

"You sure?" Kelsey asked. "What if I just throw coffee at the customers again?"

"You're one of the best I've got," Tom praised her. "The customers love you. That guy was an asshole who had it coming to him from what I heard, and he is no longer allowed in this shop."

"Thank you, and yea, I can come back now if you need, I know this was my shift," she explained.

"That's ok," Tom said. "Also, no more covering shifts for you. I found a sucker who will work any day, any time, on any notice," he laughed.

"Oh god," Kelsey laughed. "That sounds awful."

"Don't worry, he didn't seem to mind," Tom smiled.

Gerome sat down at the bar with Demetry to talk.

"How can I help?" Demetry laughed.

"I'm thinking about putting in my two weeks," Gerome explained. "I looked at some houses for rent and I might have found one we can all afford if you guys want. I just need to make sure I'm not going to end up broke if I make this choice."

155

"Oh man," Demetry said. "You're serious?"

"Well yea," Gerome laughed. "Weren't you the one who inspired me to do this."

"It's true," Demetry smiled. "I just never thought you would pick being a dirty dish washer in a band, over some corporate big shot."

"Woah, woah, woah," Gerome replied. "Who said anything about being in a band."

"I know you miss the band," Demetry laughed. "I see it in the way you jam to songs. You helped form the band and it's your spot to take."

"What about Albus?" Gerome asked. "I can't just show up and kick him out."

"He pretty much quit already. He never shows up for practice, and he's cancelled our last two shows," Demetry explained. "As far as I'm concerned he's out."

"Ok," Gerome said, "Maybe I'll think about it." He tried to hold a cool face, but it quickly broke down into a smile.

"Sureee!" Demetry laughed.

Gerome smiled.

"This really is a big commitment. You sure?" Demetry asked him seriously.

"I still have my degree and experience, so I'm not in a terrible spot if this fails," Gerome explained. "This just feels right, like it's where I'm meant to be."

"Well, if you're happy, I'm happy," Demetry said with a grin.

Ryan sat at The Coffee Hole by himself sipping his drink. The door opened, and Lindsey walked in. She found him and went to sit with him.

"Hey," he said.

"Hey," she replied dryly.

"I'm sorry," Ryan apologized. "I messed up."

"Ok," Lindsey replied in the same tone. "Thank you."

Ryan sighed. "It's more than that. I had so much going on. My parents hate everything we were trying to do."

"So they just tell you to break up with me and that's it?" she asked sharply.

"No, that's where I'm going," he explained. "I just let them ruin what we had. I'm sorry for that, I need to live my own life and not let them live it for me."

"I just wanted you to be happy," Lindsey said as her tone softened.

"I know," Ryan replied as he looked down.

"I cared so much about you," Lindsey said seriously.

"Cared?" Ryan asked sadly.

Lindsey paused. "Well I still do, I just…"

"Do you think we can fix this?" Ryan asked.

"I want to," Lindsey answered. "But I'm not sure how it's going to work if your parents hate me."

"They don't hate you," Ryan reassured her, "They just don't want me to mess up and so something that ruins my life. That's ok though, I'm moving out and getting a place with Luis. I haven't told Dad, but I'm gonna save and move out and start school." He paused. "But I'm gonna need some help…"

"Of course I'll help you, you big goof," Lindsey said with a smile. "Just please don't wake up and hate me one day." She said the last part with a serious look.

Ryan smiled. "Ok, not when I wake up, but after lunch or maybe at night is ok, right?" he asked.

Lindsey closed her eyes and sighed. Rubbing her forehead, she said, "I swear, I don't even know why I accepted your apology," and smiled.

Ryan laughed. "I'm not so bad when you get to know me."

"I think that just made it worse," Lindsey laughed. "Take me back to months ago, when it was all butterflies and sweet dates."

"Hey, I never had to see you in the mornings or bring you food on your period back then," Ryan laughed. "You're not the only one losing out on this deal."

Lindsey's eyes widened, and she looked around for a split second. "You can not just talk about my lady parts in public like that."

"And here I thought calling you ugly was gonna get me put in the dog house," Ryan said as he stood up. "Come here beautiful."

"Oh no!" she replied as she folded her arms. "I'm just some angry, ugly, hungry, period monster."

Ryan laughed. "Yes, but you're my monster," he said as he put his arms around her and kissed her on the cheek.

Chapter 28

Months passed, and seasons came and went. Alex, Gerome, Kelsey, Ryan, and all their friends were gathered to celebrate Gerome, Paul, Demetry, Digs, and Alex getting a new house together.

"This feels so surreal," Gerome said, "Just last year, life was like a totally different world."

"I guess it just goes to show you that life can throw the craziest turns at you when you least expect it," Demetry said.

"Hell yea it can," Ryan replied. "It feels like life moves so slow, then all of a sudden it takes off like a bat outta hell."

"I went from a stuff-shirt in a suit, and now I'm literally in a band that could go on tour next year," Gerome said. "How are we supposed to see this stuff coming?" he laughed.

"I guess you don't," Alex said. "I guess you're supposed to just keep moving forward and have faith that the choices you're making are the right ones."

Kelsey laughed. "Yea, I'm done pretending like I have any idea what is going on."

"Me too," Ashley laughed. "Because I know you don't have any idea what is going on."

The group started laughing.

"Hey! At least I learned how to check my email, and am passing my classes. I don't think I want to push my luck for more than that," Kelsey laughed.

"Speaking of classes," Gerome said. "How are your classes going Ryan?"

"Pretty good...ish," Ryan laughed. "Working all day and taking all these night classes can be really hard. I don't feel like I have any time to do anything after I get off at seven and have class at seven every day."

"Man, that's rough," Demetry said.

"Yea, but hell, I don't want to be the only one out of all of us that ends up falling behind," Ryan laughed. "She'll be a doctor by next year, you guys will be some famous band, you already sold a painting for how much? Ten thousand or something? I better find a new planet or something damnit!"

They all laughed, Kelsey rolled her eyes, Gerome rubbed the back of his head, and Alex smiled.

"That reminds me Mr. Painter!" Gerome said to Alex. "I never got my painting! And don't tell me you're gonna charge me because you're a big shot now."

"No way," Alex said with a smile. "A bowl of fruit, right? I can have it done by next week."

"I don't want a damn bowl of fruit," Gerome laughed.

"Hold on! I remember him being pretty adamant about the fruit," Demetry laughed.

"Oh yea he was," Alex added with a laugh.

"I think it would look nice in the living room!" Demetry said.

"Please stop this," Gerome laughed.

"It's too late, it's happening," Demetry laughed.

"Oh my god…" Gerome sighed.

Made in the USA
Middletown, DE
16 January 2018